CW01429064

Alchemy of Crystals

How to facilitate altered states,
connection with Source,
profound self healing
and journey into bliss

Raym

www.global-healing.com
inner peace-world peace

abn 19 401 091 034

Alchemy of Crystals

Global Healing
PO Box 1611
Byron Bay
NSW 2481
Australia
ph +61 (0)2 66 843 467
www.global-healing.com
First published by Global Healing 2000
Revised, updated and republished 2003, 2007, 2008, 2012, 2014, 2016, 2017

Edited by Chicchan and Valery Isherwood
Designed by Global Healing

Printed by Dark Horse print and design,
Building 62, 1140 Nepean Highway,
Mornington, VIC 3931, Australia

National library of Australia catalog-in-publication data:
Raym.
Alchemy of Crystals; How to facilitate altered states, connection with source and journey into bliss.
ISBN 0-9577935-2-9
1. Spiritualism. 2. Precious stones- therapeutic use.
3. Crystals - psychic aspects. 4. Precious stones - psychic aspects.
5. Crystals - therapeutic use. 1. Title.
135.2548

Contents

Preface

I have known Raym since 1995 as a healer and friend. I met him when, as a barrister, I was on circuit working at Byron Bay and had a Crystal Dreaming with him. I went in open minded and without expectations and the parameters of my life were forever expanded. At the conclusion of this experience I felt lighter and better than I could ever remember and I asked Raym to teach me this technique. I hasten to add that this was the first thought I had ever entertained about becoming a healer!

Since then I have found that my past career challenges were insignificant besides the all encompassing vastness of this area of expertise. It involves negotiating not only the physical and intellectual planes of ordinary life but also the emotional and spiritual ones which are less often directly and deliberately encountered.

This book is a guidebook for spiritual aspirants who are committed to personal and spiritual growth, who seek answers to the mysteries of life and its various experiences.

Once again Raym has produced a book that will make a lot of challenging concepts clear to those who never dreamt that their life path would take them over such peculiar and sometimes confronting terrain. The experiences recounted in this book can be witnessed and repeated by others, sometimes with dramatic and inevitably positive effects on the client. I have in my practice encountered many of the phenomena described in this book. If I had not, I confess that I would have trouble believing it.

I have had the good fortune to be apprenticed to Raym and I now practice these techniques, in conjunction with pranic healing, at my centre Harmony Lodge just north of Sydney.

Whilst I am committed to this work, I understand that not all modalities suit all people. In my experience there are those who cannot allow themselves to journey using these techniques, and perhaps one person in ten believes themselves to be unaffected by this experience. This does not diminish the work in my view or detract from its effectiveness the other 90% of the time.

I have witnessed Raym transform his own and many other lives, mine included, through the use of the techniques he is now releasing. Clearly he has worked with crystals and mastered crystal lore in other incarnations. He has an intuitive understanding of how to use crystals as powerful healing tools, for the highest good of all.

The shamanic journeys facilitated by this technique are often very beautiful and a joy to behold. However at times they are not for the faint hearted. This is a modality which must be used with respect and care. The facilitator of this work needs to have his or her feet firmly planted both on the earth and on the spiritual plane. There is nothing "touchy feely" about it, only a fool would trifle with the powerful forces that are at play in these sessions. However, this work can safely be approached and negotiated lovingly, when you know what you are doing. The facilitator needs to be level headed and calm, quick witted, fearless and hugely compassionate. Raym has all of these qualities and more.

I know that Raym has thought long and hard about the appropriateness of releasing these techniques to the general public rather than merely to those who seek him out to learn hands on through apprenticeship. I doubt that I would have begun this work if Raym had not been such a steadying force, reassuring me and always available to answer my endless questions.

If you are unable to have the good fortune to work with Raym directly to learn these techniques, I advise that it is highly appropriate to find a spiritual teacher, study hard, expand your consciousness, grow your energy body, clean up your karma and open yourself to opportunities for growth and for a stronger relationship with your Higher Self. Then you will be ready to use these techniques. Unfortunately we are all in a chicken and egg situation because working with these techniques achieves all of the above for the facilitator, but how to facilitate without first having these attributes?

The universe is filled with mystery and for serious seekers, many keys to inner knowledge are to be found in this book and through this work. As you explore this paradigm may God grant you healing, love, guidance, protection and the grace to solve your own mysteries.

Kim Fraser. (Shakti Durga)   February 2000.

Foreword

Like many men in their forties I was, until late 1994, as big a sceptic as you could hope to meet. My life whilst fulfilling and creative was hedonistic and I was not in any state of spiritual awareness. I was having a good time making the most of the robust physical and mental constitution I have been blessed with.

As I have described in the foreword to my previous book "Spirit Guide" I had an unexpected and unplanned interaction with spirit beings I did not believe in and had not been trying to contact.

This interaction and subsequent revelations were triggered by holding a rare crystal, which created a portal through which my consciousness shifted. My consciousness shifted out of this time space continuum and into a higher vibrational reality, where I was greeted by beings of the highest intent and purest love imaginable.

Naturally such an event turned my life upside down and thanks to the loving support of my wife and daughter I managed to remain stable and slowly grasp and integrate the awesome scale of the information which was downloaded into every cell of my being during my three day initiation.

I discovered in the weeks and months that followed that I innately know how to use crystals as the powerful healing tools that they are, for the divine highest good of all.

The development of the techniques outlined in this book was guided by my inter-dimensional friends in the spirit world. Crystal Dreaming can facilitate a deeply altered state of consciousness. In this state, after clearing all energetic blockages, connection with the source of all love and empowerment to create profound spiritual, emotional and physical self healing can manifest instantly.

All the indications I have point to the fact that now is an appropriate time to release this information. So I give you Alchemy of Crystals a book which, if you wish, will positively transform your life and the lives of those you choose to share these techniques with.

Prepare yourself for a journey into uncharted territory, where only the boldest explorers may first go themselves before returning to act as a loving guide for others. I honour your integrity in exploring this path.

Blessings, Love and Light, Raym.　　　February 2000.

Introduction

In publishing this book I introduce to the general public arcane and esoteric techniques which, if followed as instructed, will enable any one to access the higher dimensional realities in full consciousness. This book is the result of many lifetimes' experience and work here since 1994 under the guidance of my own spiritual team. I thank them all for their continuing patience and guidance.

This book contains all the tools you need to facilitate an altered state, shamanic journey or as I prefer to call it Crystal Dreaming for another person. Using the power of crystals as your allies you my create a space where others may touch the Divine, discover their life's purpose and enter a state of absolute bliss. This Alchemical transition of consciousness is a profound and powerful experience and once understood can leave no doubt in the mind of the journeyer that we are not alone, that we are in the midst of great change and that each individual has a significant part to play in this change.

This book is designed for practising therapists, spiritual seekers and healers who find themselves interacting with the spirit world. It may be used as a reference or workbook. I am not offering a game to be played at leisure or to be taken lightly. These techniques can and will affect nine out of ten subjects profoundly, do not underestimate their power. This is not a beginner's book.

There are many worthy books available on the power and application of crystals for healing self and others, I honour them and their authors. The introduction and basic level of this work is brief as there is a great deal of complementary literature available. I recommend reading books on the properties of crystals before going any further.

I recommend that anyone seriously studying this book has at least completed initiation or study of Reiki, Pranic Healing or similar healing techniques. It is appropriate to have a clear and practical understanding of how energy and intention affect our bodies, as well as some insight into the nature of Karma and our own infinite consciousness as spirit beings of light.

You have chosen this book because you are ready to understand and apply the techniques I share here. Read it from cover to cover and become fully acquainted with the range of possibilities described in the advanced section and case histories, before you embark on the facilitation of a journey yourself.

Prior study in this field may be an asset provided you are not too attached to the theories and practice you have learned so far. Your best guide is your own inner knowing, higher guidance or intuition. This system of healing relies on the fact that you do, in fact, already know all you need to know to become the powerful crystal healer you were born to be.

If possible, it is best to study these techniques with me in person.

As you practise these techniques, and your understanding grows, the clients that you attract will be appropriate to your level of skill. In fact they will often reveal to you through the challenges presented during the session your next level of skill and awareness. Whatever situation you co-create in your healing sessions you are also able to resolve and create from that a beautiful and a positive outcome for all concerned.

This Alchemical process of Crystal Dreaming will transform or lift the consciousness of an individual to higher planes of existence or dimensional realities. In so doing it is inevitable that the presence of any energies or entities not totally aligned with light become apparent. I offer you the tools in this text to successfully assist their complete and permanent journey home to light and peace. The advanced section of this book deals with a delicate area of healing much misunderstood - that is clearing, rescue work or as it is more popularly known, ghost busting.

Very few contemporary books deal with this subject thoroughly. It is a sensitive subject open to misinterpretation. The techniques included (which I have been given or rediscovered) are effective and will work every time provided your intention is clear. Without doubt if you find yourself attracting work of this nature you will assist many of our beloveds who are lost and ready to find peace.

Crystal Dreaming places the participant in an extremely sensitive and vulnerable position, the participant's journey is sacred. If you are foolish enough to consider abusing these techniques consider for a moment your own Karma and how your service to others will accelerate your own journey home to light, and ultimate power with, rather than power over.

I offer these tools to be used for the Divine highest good of all. I hereby absolve myself of all actions stemming from this work that are not totally aligned with light, selfless service and unconditional love.

The focus of all Crystal Dreaming is to facilitate a clear connection for your client with their own higher guidance through their own Higher Self and spirit team. In this state they may gain profound insights into their own life purpose. They will in so doing, be touched by unconditional love, the energy that holds the fabric of our universe together. To facilitate this experience of absolute bliss is an honour and a privilege, please respect it.

Everything I include in this book is based on my own extensive experience, none of it is theory. Read on with an open heart putting aside for the present any pre-existing theories, spiritual beliefs or concepts about the nature of the reality we all live in.

You are treading an ancient and honourable path, may you be blessed on your journey. May your light shine brightly forevermore!

Authors note revised edition 2003:

This updated edition of Alchemy of Crystals includes a whole new chapter on empowering your client, which offers food for thought for the practitioner.

In this edition I have also included some sensitive material not previously in print, which I have been teaching in person. This information is now ready to be released to a wider audience, as the need for it is apparent.

I have also included a picture of the Crystal Dreaming mandala, a synopsis of the process and more case studies. I trust this extra information will serve you well.

Raym.   September 2003.

Authors note revised edition 2007:

In this edition I have added more material which I teach in person, along with further explanation of soul families, time and space, multiple realities, parallel realities, Karma, more case studies and an updated diagram. I trust this will deepen your understanding of this technique and its application.

Raym.   September 2007.

Authors note revised edition 2012:

In this edition I have renamed and reordered all chapters, included further information for clarification, more affirmations in each chapter plus list of useful affirmations at the end of the book.

Raym.   March 2012.

Authors note revised edition 2017:

In this edition I have reordered chapters to reflect the way the process is taught in person, along with a few other updates.

Raym.   July 2017.

Chapter 1
Crystal Awareness

Crystals are full of mystery and magic. Throughout the ages, indigenous peoples, shamans and healers have valued the healing energy that may be focused through a crystal. Today, crystals form part of the healing tool box of many modern practitioners; whether they be used to lift the energy of a healing space or actually laid on clients, more and more therapists are reawakening to the power of crystals and using them in their practice as healers.

In many of the great ancient cultures, (Mayan, Celtic, Native American), crystals have been used to facilitate "altered states" of awareness. In these heightened states of awareness, the participant undertook a "shamanic journey' leaving only a small part of their awareness here, in this three dimensional reality, whilst the rest of their consciousness travelled between worlds and interacted with the spirits of their ancestors and other non-physical beings.

It is still possible today to enter these altered states and experience a shamanic journey using crystals as our allies. We can access the higher dimensional realities and as our ancestors did before us, interact with inter-dimensional or spirit beings. In so doing it is possible, with the appropriate preparation, to gain insights into our life purpose and create positive change and profound personal healing based on love and forgiveness.

Crystals are freely available in most communities. If you are drawn to them there can be little doubt that you have the ability to work with them. The ancient magic and mystery of crystals can now be revealed as we enter a time free of secrets and full of sharing.

How crystals are created

Most crystals are created by the repetitive addition of new matter to a growing crystalline mass. Some crystals are created and evolve in the molten rock or magma of the earth's interior or in the volcanic lava streams which reach the earth's surface. These minerals, which include quartz, are called magmatic or igneous. They form as this molten material cools and hardens. The atoms group together creating the geometric form which determines the shape and composition of the crystal.

Some crystals grow from vapours in vents in volcanic regions. This type of crystal includes sulphur which is condensed and solidified from hot mineralised gases from beneath the earth.

Some crystals form from water solutions or grow with the help of organisms closer to the earth's surface. These sedimentary minerals are formed by mechanical or chemical weathering. Air, water, wind and ice erode and dissolve the materials that eventually are cemented together and occasionally crystallize, like calcite.

New minerals are also formed by the re-crystallization of existing minerals under great pressure and high temperatures inside the earth. These minerals change their form undergoing structural and chemical change, creating different textures, compositions and crystals. An example of one of these metamorphic minerals is garnet.

Many people believe that crystals take thousands of years to form, some speculate that when the elements are right, crystals could form in an instant. Nobody really knows.

Origins of crystal healing

Crystals are one of the oldest inter-dimensional tools known to man, The Bible refers to crystals over two hundred times. Crystals have been used for healing purposes by many ancient civilisations. The Atlanteans used crystals to harness the Earth's energy and affect the climate. Some of this knowledge was passed on to the Ancient Egyptians, Native American, Mayans, Africans, Tibetans and Celts.

Contemporary culture is presently rediscovering the power of crystals, reawakening to the therapeutic use of crystals, stones and gems in a variety of healing modalities. It is not necessary to believe in the power of crystals to be affected by them. In the hands of a Crystal Master crystals may be used to heal body, mind, emotions and Spirit. It is possible by laying stones on and around the body to open all channels and facilitate deeply altered states of consciousness and interaction with more evolved beings. Many crystal healing techniques now being rediscovered are ancient in their origins.

Choosing crystals

Quartz crystals should be clear, or mainly clear, with no chips on any of the top edges and definitely not on the point (unless you fall in love with a crystal and wish to use it for your own personal meditation).

Numerology and symmetry are important. Always be on the lookout for the following which are easy to identify and bring with them particularly strong positive energies to your layouts.

Clear quartz:

- CHANNELLING CRYSTALS. One large prominent face has 7 edges and is symmetrical. Opposite the tip on the opposite side to the 7 sided face there should be a symmetrical triangular face. This crystal will assist with communication to higher realms and may be held in the hands.

• ISIS CRYSTALS. One prominent face has 5 sides almost triangular in appearance. Should be symmetrical. This crystal will bring with it Goddess energy and will heighten awareness of ascended beings.

• DOW CRYSTALS. 3 symmetrical 7 sided or channelling faces separated by 3 symmetrical triangles. Unifying chakras and opening to Christ consciousness. A wonderful crystal to work with, priceless.

• LASERS. Naturally formed long thin crystals with a fine point. They will focus light and healing energy with precise accuracy.

• TABULAR CRYSTALS. Crystals that are noticeably flat as if they have been squashed lengthways, good for opening channels for communication.

• WINDOW CRYSTALS. Crystals with a naturally formed diamond shaped window in the top part of the crystal, useful for personal meditation and travel through time and space.

• RECORD KEEPERS. Any crystal that has small triangles apparently raised or engraved into the surface. These have been pre-programmed with information by our Atlantean ancestors and will reveal themselves to those who are able to read them. (Illustrations at the end of this chapter).

Each of these special tools will come into your hands as you are ready to use them.

Natural and polished crystals

I prefer to use crystals that are formed naturally and have not been shaped by man. The exceptions to this are shaped wands and tumblestones. Polished generators have shiny and slightly rounded faces and have often been damaged prior to polishing. Natural crystals have waves, wiggles and dull patches on their faces and sharp edges.

As polished crystals have been worked they are more expensive than natural crystals. You may consider using a polished generator if you choose to make a wand, they are harder and chip less easily.

Yin and Yang

Very clear and bright crystals are generally considered to have strong male (yang) energy, cloudy or softer crystals are considered to hold a more feminine (yin) energy. You may consider looking for crystals that have a combination of both energies (eg: a clear bright tip with a cloudy base).

Rainbow

I consider any bright clear crystal that holds within it a clearly visible rainbow spectrum to be very valuable for meditation and healing. These crystals are said to be valued by Australian Aboriginal shamans. A combination of rainbow and Dow, Isis or channelling crystal would be an exceptional find and worth acquiring. The rainbow captured within a crystal is a clear embodiment of full spectrum of energy that clear quartz emanates and harmonises.

Other crystals

All other varieties of crystals should appear clear and bright, and should clearly show within them the elements they possess - eg. iron tiger (mara mamba) should have clearly visible bands of hematite, tiger's eye and red jasper.

Colour should be strong and not grey-looking or washed-out. Always allow your intuition to guide you when buying crystals. My hands, apparently of their own accord have picked perfect dows from the special or sale tray at the wholesalers. Expect the unexpected, your guides will help, be receptive and alert when shopping for crystals.

Crystals are seductive. Beware of spending too much too fast on crystals. Take your time, those that are meant for you will always be there for you.

Cleansing Crystals

Crystals are like sponges or tape recorders, they absorb the energy of those who handle them. Many people will have touched any crystal you buy from a shop. All crystals must be cleansed before use without exception. Those that have been placed on the body or handled by others must be cleansed between sessions.

First cleansing

On purchasing a crystal, I suggest the following methods of cleansing. For the harder crystals only ie. quartz, obsidian, hematite etc, you may prepare a solution of proportionally one tablespoon of sea salt and one tablespoon of apple cider vinegar per one litre of water. Place the crystals in the solution, the crystals should be fully immersed (preferably not touching) for about 15 minutes, they can then be rinsed thoroughly and are ready to use. If you are a pranic healer or Reiki channel you may also scan them with prana to ensure they are clean.

For the softer crystals eg. fluorite, calcite, tourmaline etc, briefly rinse under cold running water then "smudge" them with a smudge stick or use sandalwood incense. Leave them in bright sunlight (after drying them) for a day or completely cover them top and bottom with dry rock salt.

As a simple general rule do not immerse crystals that end in "-ite" in water or salt water.

Subsequent cleansing, cleaning between sessions

Between sessions all crystals that have been placed on the body should be *briefly* immersed in clean (not salty) water and white prana or Reiki energy scanned over the crystals until you are satisfied they are cleansed. You may also choose to blow light through each crystal as you dry it. Do this by drawing in light through the crown and consciously blowing it out of your mouth into the crystal.

Programming Crystals

Crystals may be programmed to do all sorts of useful things. For the purposes of healing, I suggest all crystals are programmed to bring in Divine love, light, Christ consciousness and healing energy. Crystals are programmed after thorough cleaning and you may use the following technique.

Sit for 3 to 5 minutes holding the crystal in front of your heart chakra sending it unconditional love (you may gently massage the crystal with pure Frankincense or Sandalwood oil whilst you are doing this). When you feel comfortable with the crystal and in tune with it hold it up to your third eye and send it a clear and simple picture of what you want it to do. Ask it to work with you with love and for the Divine highest good of all. And so, until you reprogramme it, the crystal will continue to do as you will, even after repeated cleansing.

Programming most applies to clear quartz. Other crystals have their own strong vibration and a clear purpose which is already part of their reason for being and I find no need to programme them.

Sacred geometry, numerology, patterns and glyphs

The patterns and numbers of crystals that you place around the client's body can have a profound effect on the energies you invite into your healing space. These patterns may relate to sacred geometry, the flower of life, magic squares, ancient sacred symbols known as sigls or glyphs or the Quabalistic tree of life. All separate areas of study in their own right.

If you choose to pursue these areas of study I suggest that you find a wholesome and loving teacher, if you decide to experiment alone, proceed with caution. By calling in these energies you give them permission to enter your sacred healing space.

Conclusion

Now you have a basic understanding of crystals and how to cleanse them, we will in the next chapter look at how the energies of different crystals affect the human energy or chakra system. The focus in Crystal Dreaming is on using crystals to cleanse, balance and harmonise a persons energy field, whilst also opening the higher chakras to an influx of spiritual energy in order to access an altered state of consciousness.

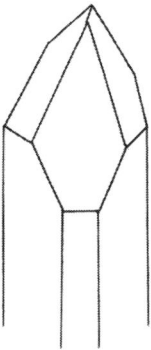

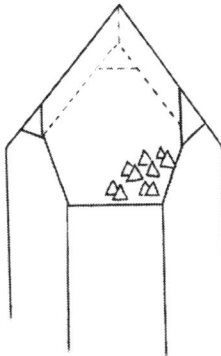

Isis **Channeller with record keepers** **Window**

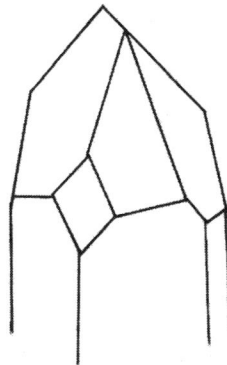

Chapter 2
Crystals and chakras

Crystal healing is a form of vibrational medicine. As all things constantly vibrate and interrelate, crystals when placed on the body, can positively affect the energy centres (chakras) or organs beneath them. All naturally formed crystals or stones have an energy that you can feel if you create the still space to do so. This energy is inherent in the stone and relates to its colour as well as the minerals that comprise it and the way it was formed. You are the best judge of how different stones affect your energy and with practice and observation how they effect the emotional, physical, mental and spirit bodies of others. A few gifted people have researched this area of energy and crystals thoroughly and I recommend further reading.

In Crystal Dreaming the focus is accessing an altered state. Harmonising, aligning and balancing the chakras in order to facilitate an uninterrupted, free flow and grounding of Spiritual Energy into this present time and space, assists this process. Other worthy crystal healing systems focus on the healing power of stones when placed on organs, secondary chakras and areas of disease. In this system of Crystal Dreaming we deal with imbalances by accessing the superconscious and Higher Self to achieve understanding and remedy. Therefore in Crystal Dreaming our primary focus is on how laying stones *around* the body may facilitate an altered state. We may also during this process place stones on the main chakras, so an awareness of how various stones affect these chakras is appropriate.

I offer a brief list of some readily available crystals and their properties, your own personal research and practice will reveal a great deal more.

Some commonly used stones and their properties.

Amazonite	Inspiring, nurturing, assists self expression
Amber	Uplifting, joyful, revitalising, energising, protective
Amethyst	Calming, protective, spiritual awareness, purifying
Ametrine	Male/female balance, blockage clearer
Angelite	Opens to higher realms, soft, light
Aquamarine	Reassuring, shields from negativity, Atlantean
Aventurine	
-green	Tranquil, balancing, positive, heart opening
Bloodstone	Gives strength and stamina, clears self-doubt
Calcite-gold	Alert, clarifies third eye vision, energises, revitalises
Calcite-clear	Clear vision, astral projection
Carnelian	Creativity, vitality, trauma easer, stabiliser

Alchemy of Crystals

Celestite	Divine expression, calming connection to etheric
Chrysocolla	Creative expression, auric cleanser, feminine
Chrysoprase	Anxiety reliever, compassion, equilibrium
Citrine	Vitality, abundance, clarity, cleanser
Danburite	Universal love, Angelic vibration
Elestial	Magical, clear connection to higher dimensions
Emerald	Tonic, strengthens immune system, heart opener
Fluorite-purple	Opens to higher levels, clarity, access to spirit, protective
Garnet	Love, grounding, stimulates kundalini
Hematite	Grounds, protects, energises, balances
Herkimer	
Diamond	Clairvoyance, psychic, telepathic clarity
Howlite	Eases pain and stress, calming
Iron Tiger	Grounds creativity, spirituality, motivator, protects
Jade	Stability, calming, past life recall
Jasper-red	Nurturing, grounding, stabilising
Kyanite	Communication, high vibration, spiritual meditation
Labrodite	Access Akashic records, spirituality, intuition, strength
Lapis Lazuli	Cleanser, protects, access to spirit, ancient Egypt
Larimar	Peaceful communication, nurturing, high vibration
Lepidolite	Opens to self-love, transition, alleviates stress
Malachite	Incisive, breaks limitations, releases emotional pain
Moldavite	Starseed/ET origins, catalyst, interstellar gateway
Moonstone	Feminine, emotional release and balancer
Obsidian	
-black	Opens inner depths, clears negativity, protecting
-snowflake	Absorbs negativity and pain, grounds and balances
-green	Attracts/releases negative energy, heart cleanser
Peacock Ore	Soothing, calming, mind clearer
Pyrite	Grounds spiritual, opens psychic channels
Quartz	
-clear	Amplifies light, healing, inter-dimensional link
-rose	Love, forgiveness, compassion, gentle, nurturing
-rutilated	Stimulates life-force, eases depression, manifestation
-smokey	Grounding, relaxing, sexual balancer
-spirit	Connection to higher realms, harmony, unity
-titanium	Bridge between worlds, strengthens aura, way shower
-tourmilanated	Protects, removes/transmutes negativity, spell breaker
Rhodocrosite	Compassion, Divine love
Ruby	Strength, self-confidence, helps immune system

Sapphire	Inter-dimensional communication, psychic, spiritual
Selenite	Connects to spiritual plane, Christ consciousness
Sodalite	Grounding, cleansing, calming
Tektite	Expanding consciousness, clears chakras
Tiger Eye	Strength and fearlessness, personal power
Topaz-clear	Uplifting, opens consciousness/awareness of spirit
Tourmaline	
-black	Grounding, memory stimulator, absorbs pain
-green	Heart opening, healing and releasing
-pink	Opens heart to joy, releases grief
Turquoise	Self-expression, balance, peace, nurtures
Unakite	Heart balancer, self-love and confidence

There is extensive information available about healing stones and their properties in many other worthy books. My recommendation is that you keep your initial tool box of crystals fairly small. Beware of overloading your conscious mind with too much information. Better to acquire the stones, sit with them and sense their energy and how you, special person that you are, will use them in your healings.

Be bold, be adventurous and above all else, always work with love in your heart. It is your clear will and focus to be a pure channel of love and light that is the most important factor in any healing you may undertake.

The Human Aura or energy field

All living humans are surrounded by an aura or energy field, it extends for about a metre around the human body and its condition can tell a healer much about a person's state of health. The aura can be felt using the hands, it can be seen by clairvoyants, and it can be perceived by using a pendulum.

Chakras

Chakras are spinning energy centres or vortexes within the aura and close to the body. The 7 main chakras closest to the body are situated at the crown (top of head), the third eye (centre of forehead, just above the eyes), the throat, the heart (centre of chest), the solar plexus, the sacral (navel), and the root (base of spine), there are also chakras at the rear of those mentioned. Each one relates to different aspects of the etheric body. They are real and tangible.

Whilst the most commonly used term for these energy centres is Asian or Indian in origin, knowledge of these centres was not confined to the East. The Ancient Celts and Druids referred to these centres as the Seven Seals, and initiates knew how to diagnose and treat illnesses through chakra awareness.

The state of a person's chakras reveals a great deal to a trained therapist.

They can, with a patient's permission, be manipulated by a healer, they can be unblocked, cleaned and re-energised. Any potential physical illness will manifest as an imbalance in the auric field or as a chakra blockage before it manifests physically, therefore these methods of healing are also excellent preventative medicine.

Chakras and Crystal Dreaming™

In the Crystal Dreaming crystal layout, we are working with the 7 bodily chakras plus 2 above the head and 1 below the feet, a total of 10 chakras. A brief description of their function and some examples of stones you may place on these chakras follows. I will cover the complete Crystal Dreaming mandala later.

Stellar Gateway, colour opalescent rainbow

About one metre above the head on a centre line with the body is the Stellar Gateway, the umbilical cord that connects us to the spirit realm and oneness. An elestial crystal may be placed here.

Soul Star, colour opalescent magenta

About 15cm above the head is the soul star which integrates unconditional love from the heart with the spirit. Selenite may be placed here.

Crown Chakra, colour clear white

Centre top of head, gateway to the Higher Self, universal consciousness. Clear quartz may be placed here.

Third Eye Chakra, colour violet

Centre of forehead. Place of visions, perceptions, seeing other realities, intuition, inner senses. Amethyst may be placed here.

Throat Chakra, colour turquoise

Hollow of sternum, base of throat. Centre of expression, self-regulation through thyroid, communication. Turquoise may be placed here.

Heart Chakra, colour green, pink or blue

Centre of chest. Centre of feeling, holding place for all past feelings, devotion, healing. Rose quartz may be placed here.

Solar plexus Chakra, colour yellow

Between the sternum and navel closer to the heart chakra. In the moment emotions, personality, power centre. Citrine may be placed here.

Sacral Chakra, colour orange

Just below the navel. Creativity, sexuality, vitality, sensuality, enthusiasm.

Carnelian may be placed here.

Root Chakra, colour red

Base of spine. Anchors the spirit to the material world and body to the Earth. Red jasper may be placed here.

Earth Star, colour black

20cm below the feet. Anchor to the earth plane. Hematite, iron tiger or black obsidian may be placed here.

Conclusion

In Crystal Dreaming we do not use stones to treat specific ailments, rather we create a state where any client can diagnose and treat their own challenges by aligning the chakras, entering an altered state of awareness and accessing the superconscious.

Having an understanding of how crystals may affect your client you are now ready to study the unique crystal layout used in Crystal Dreaming, which will safely trigger an expanded state of consciousness for your client.

Chapter 3
Your Crystal Dreaming™ Mandala

You will need about 3.5 metres of floor space in a North-South aspect. *The client's head always points towards magnetic north* as you wish to harmonise with natural planetary energies. Prepare your crystal room prior to your session by clearing yourself then the space and laying out these cleansed and programmed crystals, around the shape that your client's body will fill. I advise working on a futon or foam mattress on the floor.

Above the head

All crystals with points should point towards the centre of the client's head, which is always pointing as close to magnetic North as possible.

Starting around one metre above the top of the head on a centre line with the body, place the following crystals on the floor going down towards the crown:

- A clear quartz ball (4 cm diameter or larger, with rainbow inclusions, if possible) on a centre line with the body, around 1m above the head

- A similar sized elestial crystal corresponding to the stellar gateway.

- A Lemurian crystal.

- A large tabular quartz, preferably a Dow, Channelling, or Isis crystal.

- A clear quartz wand or quality quartz points, as available

- A selenite wand, preferably natural.

- Kyanite wand, preferably natural.

- A pointed piece of fishtail selenite (about 15cm above the head above the crown corresponding to soul star chakra).

- Two lasers either side of the fishtail selenite.

- Two natural amethyst terminators or clusters either side of them.

- Titanium coated quartz or natural rainbow quartz pointing through a large natural fluorite octahedron (if possible) close to the crown.

- Left and right hand window crystals close to the centre line either side of the crown (preferred but not essential, quartz will suffice).

Around the crown

All crystals point towards the centre of the head arranged in a fan or several fans around the top of the head, either side of your centre line of crystals. All are close to the head.

  • Six natural *purple* fluorite octahedrons, three either side of the head. All *purple* fluorite octahedrons have clear quartz points behind them pointing through the octahedrons, amplifying each piece, pointing into the centre of the head.

  • Additional smaller natural *purple* fluorite octahedrons as close to the head as possible, all amplified by smaller clear quartz points.

  • Clear quartz points and/or clusters as many as you see fit, fanned around the head all pointing to the centre of the head.

Behind the neck

  • A 3cm diameter *purple* fluorite ball, egg, heart or tumbler is placed behind the clients head in the hollow part of the neck at the base of the skull.

Below the feet

  • About 20cm below and on a centre line with the feet in alignment with the Earth Star chakra a 4cm or larger diameter hematite, black obsidian or iron tiger ball.

  • About 10cm either side of each foot, two or three hematite or iron tiger tumblers each side, to be placed closer to or on the body as needed when dealing with a particularly ungrounded client.

See diagram Crystal Dreaming Mandala at the end of this book.

Chapter 4
The spirit world

The aim of any Crystal Dreaming session is for your client to personally access their own higher guidance, the superconscious, oneness and bliss, through a safely expanded state of consciousness, in a nurturing space.

In this drug-free and no-touch process, your client remains fully clothed. Any energies not totally aligned with light and unconditional love will become apparent in the session. If they are a sentient being they will do their best to stop the process as it threatens their tenure with your client. This is a normal experience and I cover how we deal with this at length later in this book.

When your client establishes a clear and direct channel themselves to their own spiritual team then they may resolve challenges on the spiritual, emotional and physical level instantaneously. However, Crystal Dreaming may not be as effective a healing process where there is mental instability. When we access altered states of consciousness we do it through a stable and co-operative mind or mental body. Do not offer this process to anyone who appears to be mentally unstable or has had a recent psychotic episode.

When in communication with your Higher Self or other evolved and loving spirit beings it is possible to gain an overview of life's challenges, discover what your life's purpose is and activate your blueprint or life plan. This makes Crystal Dreaming an ideal experience for the spiritual seeker.

In order to guide your client effectively through the spiritual realm you will need to understand more about that reality and the beings your client may meet and interact with on the spiritual plane.

You are a sovereign being of Light

It is really important that you understand and believe to your core this universal truth, because when you do, your client gets it too.

We are all parts of a much bigger individual and group consciousness. Our experience here on Earth is a very small part of what we actually are experiencing all the time. We are enormous, powerful and unbelievably beautiful beings that exist in a state of constant bliss. Our consciousness is infinite and we can tap into it through this process. Most people do not understand this as most of us most of the time feel that our experience here is all that we are. It is in fact a *part* of what we are.

When we experience the illusion of mortality here on Earth we believe we are limited, when in fact we are limitless. As sovereign beings of Light and unconditional love we can only be affected by what we choose or allow. This is a powerful key to unlocking all sorts of challenging situations uncovered through Crystal Dreaming.

Remember, at all times in a session both for you and your client, nothing has power over us unless we allow it.

The Spirit world and interacting with spirit beings

There is a source of unconditional love from which we all spring, of which we are all part and to which we all eventually return. That consciousness exists in all beings throughout the Universe whether they are aware of it or not. Without exception on this plane, we are all spirits having a human experience. Our consciousness or spirit always was and always will be; we do not "die" when our physical body ceases to function, our awareness continues, shifting into a higher dimension, eventually returning to the Source and becoming one with All There Is.

Earth is a most volatile and beautiful planet, a dense and sensual planet, most of whose occupants become separated from their awareness of Oneness soon after arrival. We live in an experiential school, where we learn to evolve as beings of love. We learn how to balance spiritually with our existence on the physical plane. We learn about light and dark, love and fear, pain and joy, separation from and oneness with our own inherent divinity.

We repeatedly reincarnate on Earth until we reach Enlightenment or Mastery and no longer need to return in a physical body. Many souls become trapped in this cycle of death and rebirth by Karma (see below) and attachment to the sensual pleasures available here on the Earth plane, losing track of their Divine plan or their reason for coming here.

Many confused souls also get trapped in the Earth's energy fields, reluctant or fearful to leave, experiencing a form of purgatory known as the Astral or lower 4th dimension. Beings in this zone frequently manifest as ghosts or earthbound spirits in their futile attempts to re-enter this third dimensional reality they have become so attached to.

There are many other planets and dimensional realities in the Universe which are inhabited by intelligent and evolved civilisations. Many of these civilisations have evolved beyond the limitations of the physical third dimension, therefore, unless they choose to lower their vibration, they are not visible to our human eyes. They may however become clearly visible and we may interact with them by lifting our vibration and entering the altered state facilitated through Crystal Dreaming.

Time and space

Linear time is an illusion. Our higher consciousness exists constantly in a never ending now, in no time-space, in a state of absolute bliss. We can access this state through Crystal Dreaming.

By accessing no time-space we effectively access *all time-space.* To do this in full consciousness is a profound experience, where incredible and miraculous things may occur, provided it is accessed with the guidance of a trained Crystal Dreaming practitioner.

Without training and initiation, it is challenging for our minds and ego to grasp this concept of non-linear time and space, so for ease of understanding I describe events generally in a linear, earthly time line. Bear in mind however, as you train and practice that there are multiple realities that your client may experience and linear time is a third dimensional illusion.

Higher Self

The higher or main part of our individuated consciousness exists in a blissful state in a never ending now. When we call on and meet our Higher Self (which can be male or female) we are met by a radiant and beautiful being of light, ourselves as we truly are. Our Higher Selves are experiencing multiple realities simultaneously and their consciousness is limitless.

Our limited consciousness here may be just one of many experiences we are having now. When we access our Higher Self as well as finding out why we came here and how things are going, we may also merge with our own Higher Consciousness for a short period.

Merging can be an awesome experience for your client, particularly those who are experiencing fear based challenges on this plane, because they see how small and surmountable these challenges are. Clients may experience a state of bliss which is so vast, peaceful and joy filled as to defy description.

Soul family

We all belong to a group of souls that repeatedly incarnate together over many lifetimes. Within that group we may have experienced being spouse, brother, sister, parent, best friend, etc. So you may have incarnated many times with those closest to you in this life.

Members of your soul family who are not incarnated may also be your spirit guides. As they (your Higher Self and other discarnate beings) exist in a never ending now, they just "wait" until all the members of the soul family have left their bodies, then get together and plan the next group incarnation.

Twin Flames

Within any soul family there may be twin flames, beings who have a very long standing and deep love between them. A love which has been experienced and re-experienced over many lifetimes. Because of the deep love these beings feel for each other they may volunteer to incarnate as the most annoying and apparently hurtful person in your life, in order to teach you and help you grow. They may also incarnate as the deepest and most profound love of your life.

Multiple simultaneous incarnations on Earth

Your Higher Self may be having several incarnations simultaneously here on Earth now. It is rarely necessary for you to meet the young African boy or the elderly Greek lady who are also aspects of your Higher Self, alive on this planet at the same time as you are.

Multiple realities, parallel realities

Our Higher Selves may also be experiencing several incarnations in different realities, not necessarily on this planet, simultaneously. Trauma from those experiences can affect us here and now and may present for release in any session.

Oneness

It is important to understand that ultimately we are all one consciousness, not just us human beings but all beings. In fact all things are one unified consciousness. You may assist your clients to experience this in any Crystal Dreaming session; however most people experience this earthly reality and higher realities in a separated state of consciousness. Therefore whilst we understand that we are all one we also accept that during any Crystal Dreaming session, most of the time, most of the beings we interact with, in this and on other planes, exist as a completely separate consciousness to us - as separate as I appear to be from you.

Spirit guides

In choosing to incarnate on Earth, a spirit draws up a life-plan or blueprint: if s/he follows it, s/he will evolve to their maximum potential in that lifetime and may not therefore need to return to this reality in physical form. Before incarnating, a spirit makes an agreement with their soul family, friends, ancestors and other loving spirit beings on the higher dimensional levels, that they will assist, monitor and guide them through the coming lifetime. These friends are commonly referred to as "spirit guides."

Every living person has spirit guides, without exception.

- Spirit guides are evolved spirits who are in service to humanity, assisting with an individual's growth and enriching their own experience in the process.

- Spirit guides are *always* positive and loving and are *always* focused on the Divine highest good of the person whom they have agreed to help.

- Spirit guides are ready, willing and able to assist in any healing, provided it is for the Divine highest good of the person they are helping and permission is given for them to intercede.

- It is appropriate to treat guides with love and respect. Be polite, clear and loving in your dealing with them, they are your equal.

It is vital that you understand, when interacting with these and inter-dimensional beings, that you are communicating with other sentient beings. These beings are not an aspect of your client's subconscious or a figment of their imagination. You are accessing the superconscious and in so doing are interacting with other evolved intelligent beings that are as separate from your client as you are from them.

Through Crystal Dreaming it is possible to contact and have a dialogue with those in the spirit world and in other planes of existence throughout time-space. Please undertake a solemn promise now that you will always use these techniques only for the Divine highest good of yourself and those you choose to work with. *Never* use these techniques lightly or as a game and always affirm that you are using them in accordance with the Divine plan.

Ancestors

As well as our guides we may also be assisted by our ancestors. This is particularly true of contemporary indigenous tribal cultures, such as African, Aboriginal, Indian, Maori, Fijian, Hawaiian etc. Ancestors, like guides, are here to help us. Within your clients ancestry there may be a medicine man or woman or a shaman. These spirit beings can assist in resolving challenges that may be pertinent to your client's cultural background.

Spiritual teacher

We all have a spiritual teacher; a loving being who has been our friend and mentor for many incarnations. If your client has accepted a teacher or guru in this lifetime they may be surprised to discover that their spiritual teacher is not the same person.

Our teacher has an intimate understanding of our soul's journey and what we set out to achieve on this plane this time around. He or she is in a great position to offer guidance and advice. Teachers come from many traditions, times and places. One thing is for sure, you will have spent at least one lifetime incarnated with them.

27

Angels

We are all also surrounded by angels, non-physical beings with a particular interest in this planet. They frequently appear as winged light beings and may act as protectors and guides. Angels have never incarnated in the flesh as we do.

Ascended Masters

Human beings are able to reach a state of Mastery in which they become complete embodiments of their higher selves. They live in a state of unconditional love and in service to the whole of humanity. Past Masters include Buddha, Jesus, Quan Yin, the Lady Nada and St. Germain. When these masters leave this plane they have no need to return in the flesh but may continue their service to humanity as Ascended Masters. They are spirit beings with a great understanding of this planet and all of its fear based challenges. As such they are a great help to our evolution as a species. Each of us has a personal connection with a particular Ascended Master. Their guidance is invaluable.

Ancient Gods and Goddesses

Your client may encounter one of the great ancient gods and goddesses, such as Isis, Zeus or Sekhmet. Be aware that these beings may not love your client unconditionally and your client may have an ancient agreement to serve them. Find out as much as you can about their relationship and what the god/goddess wants before you allow them to direct your clients actions or speak through your client.

Karma

We are all subject to the laws of Karma. Before being born here we agree to personally re-experience in subsequent lives, any pain or suffering we may cause for any other being, in this life.

If you hurt someone *deliberately,* physically or emotionally and it is not part of their Divine plan, then in your next incarnation you will experience the same kind of pain you inflicted previously, on another.

This knowledge, when you truly understand it is very liberating, and it affects all your actions. The challenge is that we pass through many lifetimes blissfully unaware of the ramifications of our actions, hence we may get caught up on the wheel of Karma, clearing Karma in one life only to create more through our ignorance, in the next.

Earth and her Consciousness

Our Earth is experiencing a great transition. She is a beautiful intelligent living being who loves us all dearly. We are a unique and diverse planet going through great changes. Earth welcomes love and honouring from us; give thanks every day for all the beautiful creatures, plants and weather she sustains us with. Thank also the Aboriginal ancestors and nature spirits who also watch over her.

We all have a duty of care to our host as a species and as individuals. As mass consciousness has a profound effect on our reality, lifting individual consciousness will affect our reality en masse. Global Healing and the evolution of the species therefore starts with the individual, you and your clients.

Shifts happen

Earth is about to reach the end of a great cosmic cycle and as a natural result of that, she is changing, she is shifting awareness and density. It is vital that we shift with her, and assist as many other souls as possible to access their own inherent power as divine beings of love through Crystal Dreaming.

Accessing our blueprint

Each one of us has a blueprint or life-plan that is part of the raising of mass consciousness and planetary healing. Through Crystal Dreaming we are able to assist the recall of that blueprint by first clearing negative energies and entities and then introducing our clients to their spirit guides, Higher Self, Guardian Angel, spiritual teacher, Ascended Master or other highly evolved loving beings.

This interaction then leads to an understanding of their own life purpose. Through sharing and practising Crystal Dreaming techniques you will contribute to an exponential growth of consciousness which will enable the whole species to make a smooth transition into the higher dimensional love based realities.

Conclusion

You now have a basic outline of the area you will be exploring with clients. In the next chapter we will look at the most common phenomena you will encounter through Crystal Dreaming.

Chapter 5
Entities

As there are loving, intelligent, highly evolved spirits, so there are less intelligent, less evolved, less loving spirits and spirit beings. These are *never* spirit guides. These less evolved beings, often described as negative entities, inhabit the lower fourth dimension. They may be simple forms of negative energy that have become self aware, they may be simple beings created by misguided individuals seeking to exert power over others or they may be ancient fear based beings who have lost their awareness of their own connection with the light. They are most frequently Earthbound spirits; people who do not realise they are dead. They are often confused or fearful and sometimes angry, anger being a manifestation of fear. Remember to be compassionate when dealing with an angry being - they are afraid.

It is normal for clients to become aware of, and with your help, release entities during a Crystal Dreaming session, the most common being Earthbound spirits or dead people. In fact it would be unusual for any session not to include this experience.

Where do they get their energy?

Entities attach themselves to a person in a time of need and their presence is common. These beings will make an agreement with that person, usually on a subconscious level, to reassure them in a moment of fear or panic, provided they can stay with them. Many simple entities and Earthbound spirits seek the comfort of being with a living person who is experiencing life, love and happiness on this plane.

Others feed off the negative emotions generated by their host and enjoy experiencing the sensuality of life on this plane experiencing life vicariously through their host. They encourage their host through their emotional body to create personally disempowering situations, reaffirming the reason for the entities presence (reassurance, "protection," etc) and thus the entities secure tenure. They may also amplify simple fears or encourage the host to take part in any activity that gives pleasure to the entity.

Spirit Attachment

Confused dead people are the common form of entity you will encounter. Any form of attachment will stifle both the host's and the attached spirit's growth. The attached spirit remains trapped in the lower fourth dimension although it feels more comfortable experiencing three dimensional sensations through its unwitting host.

The host will be impelled by the spirit not to grow or develop in any way that would create a feeling of independence or freedom in the host, and thus threaten the tenure of the spirit attached to that person. The host will be encouraged to continue behaviour patterns that subjugate and disempower them. Any person with any spirit attachments will be prevented from accessing their own spirit guides by that attachment.

Occasionally desperate or cheeky earthbound spirits may pretend to be a person's spirit guide. Guides are utterly selfless and not remotely interested in earthly pleasures, earthbound spirits are the opposite.

As all spirit attachments are earthbound they are all still very much subject to the desires and needs of a three dimensional experience. They are often lost and confused souls, occasionally lovers from past lives that have waited for sometimes hundreds of years for their loved one to reincarnate, only to find that their loved one is now a different sex and does not remember them.

Spirits may remain attached to a person for an entire lifetime without detection. They will leave, desperately looking for a new host, on the host's death bed. The attached spirit will have prevented the host fulfilling their life purpose, although apart from some odd personal habits the situation would not attract undue attention.

How a spirit attaches itself to your client

In the majority of cases you are likely to encounter, most of the opportunities for attachment will have been created on a subconscious level by your client. A spirit needs the permission of the subject in order to attach itself to her/him. This often happens early in the client's life when they experience extreme trauma on an emotional level. This often goes hand in hand with physical pain or emotional abuse.

I include here many of the circumstances that create an opportunity for a spirit to attach to someone.

- A child is neglected or abused, or is left alone for long periods of time. The child starts to ask the Universe for help, they do not understand why such an awful thing could happen to them. They ask either out loud or subconsciously for company or help and solace. A presence arrives and offers just that, provided they can stay with them. This may happen as a feeling or through a dream, either way the child consents and the agreement is made and holds until it is dissolved.

- A person becomes genuinely fearful whilst watching a horror movie. That deep seated fear creates a powerful need to ask for help. "Can someone please stop me feeling like this?" There is a response from an earthbound spirit and the agreement is made.

• A soldier in World War two cradles his mate in his arms as he dies, his mate is desperate fearful and in pain. The soldier promises his dying friend with all his heart, "I'll never leave you mate", his mate thanks him and dies. The soldier himself is killed shortly afterwards, with his promise fixed in his mind, he refuses the opportunity to transit and starts looking for his mate. His mate has transited and after a life review is reincarnated, the soldier finds his mate even though he might now be a woman and as they have a prior agreement he reunites with his old friend.

• Two spinster sisters live together and care for each other into old age. They promise always to look after each other and never leave each other. The first to die refuses transit and sticks around to look after her sister. By the time the second sister dies she has forgotten the promise or is looking forward to seeing her dead sister in heaven. The first sister waits until her sister is reincarnated, possibly as a man, and as she already has permission attaches herself to him in order to fulfil her promise to always look after her.

• A young couple deeply in love, live in an age and era where their love is forbidden. They are forcibly separated, but before separating they promise to love each other always. The woman is forced to marry and eventually has children and begins to like her husband who although much older is a kind and generous man. She is forbidden to enquire about her young lover who is many miles away. Slowly she forgets their promise, she dies in childbirth and transits peacefully. Her lover's life is different, he lives only for reunification with his lover, he tries everything he can to see her but fails. He tries to start a new life but is obsessed with her, he dies a sad and lonely death. He refuses transit preferring to look for his lover. He looks for several generations until she reincarnates, he finds her and as there is a prior agreement he attaches to her.

• A little boy is out playing on his tricycle when he is run down by a car. The suddenness of his death catches his guides unaware. He is confused and becomes frightened of them, they can not help him if he does not let them. He looks for someone like his mum or dad and makes an agreement with them in a dream.

- A young woman plays with a Ouija board with her friends, having no idea that the "game" she is playing is allowing an Earthbound spirit to attach itself to her. She does not realise that the psychic powers she gains after the seance come at a price.

In all cases of past life agreements until your client is in an altered state they will have no conscious recall of making the agreement, or the past life in which they made it.

Why is Spirit Attachment a serious matter?

Spirit attachment is a serious situation for your client as it drives an energetic wedge between them and their own spirit guides and Higher Self. This therefore leads to a deviation from their life's purpose. Any intuition felt by the subject will be motivated by the interests of their attached earthbound spirits, who are neither aware of nor focused on your client's life plan. This may also lead to your client falling far short of their potential in this life.

Fortunately it is easy to help out both the earthbound spirit and the client, which is what this section will cover. You will if you choose, in due course, be able to assist in cases of attachment and possession.

How do I deal with them?

Spirit attachment and negative entities are a very common phenomena and Crystal Dreaming by its nature will reveal all forms of negative attachment. Some entities are just lost and confused, some may behave like beloved children having a tantrum. They should at all times be treated politely, kindly and firmly. Never allow yourself to be intimidated by them and do not take any nonsense from them. Crystal Dreaming offers ways of helping these confused beings find peace with ease and grace.

Many entities you deal with will be Earthbound Spirits, those who have become confused or lost after (an often traumatic) death. Listen to their stories then help them understand they are dead, they will be stuck in the year they died - so ask them what year it is. Explain that their bodies are long gone and that it is time for them to find peace, they can stop being in pain now.

With their permission, when they are ready, have your client call on their spirit guides three times.

"I call on this person's spirit guides, I call on this person's spirit guides, I call on this person's spirit guides.

Please come close to us and help this person journey home to light and find peace. Now."

Encourage them to leave with them, more on this later.

In the early stages of your learning and practice you may work with another student for support. If you encounter a stubborn negative entity and you feel intimidated or overwhelmed, you may bring the session to a close and refer your client to a more experienced practitioner. Remember however that your clients are guided to you and your team would not present you with anything you could not deal with.

Ideally you should have supervision or expert training for clearing the more challenging entities. I suggest that you seek personal training from myself or one of my authorised teachers. If one is not available in your area and you feel guided to do this work, you will be working from the advanced section of this book. Study and become familiar with the whole Crystal Dreaming process. Learn all the affirmations in the advanced section off by heart. Be very aware of everything you verbalise during a session particularly a clearing. Think before you speak, proceed with patience, caution and a loving heart.

How do entities affect a Crystal Dreaming™ journey?

Entities will block a person's connection with their own spirit guides. Until the attached being or entity is escorted safely home to light, your client cannot work directly and clearly with their guides, Higher Self, teacher or Ascended Master. Therefore Crystal Dreaming may not be productive unless you release any entity as soon as you encounter it.

Chapter 6
Your preparation

The Alchemical process of Crystal Dreaming will shift your client's consciousness into an altered state or higher dimensional reality where they will connect with their own higher guidance in full consciousness and with full recall. You will be creating a sacred space for your client to experience a special journey into bliss, a journey that will act as a very positive and memorable catalyst in their lives. Each journey is unique and no matter how many journeys you may eventually facilitate, remember that for your client it will be a unique and very special experience.

Your team

You are a valuable member of a team. You ask for your own guides, teachers and friends to help out with the healing process and you are a vital link between the spirit world, other higher dimensional realities and this third dimension. Give credit where credit is due, acknowledge your team and remind yourself and others that you have the privilege of acting as a third dimensional team member and conduit for light on this plane.

Always thank your team after a session and give them verbal acknowledgement in front of your client, it is a team effort.

My approach

There are many ways to use crystals in healing. I describe here one particular method which in its nature may encompass aspects of spiritual or crystal healing. As your client gains access to their own higher guidance so they are able to diagnose and treat their own imbalances, either directly or through lifestyle changes. They have only to ask and they will be given valuable information on life purpose, diet, exercise, relationships, finances, career, etc and helped with an influx of healing energy from their own team, providing they give their permission for this to happen.

Your client comes to you in trust and it is your responsibility to ensure the area you work in is cleansed and protected. You are opening all their psychic channels simultaneously. If you are lax in your preparation your client could experience psychic attack or spirit attachment during your session. There are many misguided beings who would enjoy the opportunity to access and interfere with a vulnerable person, so take care and time in preparing yourself and your healing space thoroughly before your client arrives.

All cleansing and protection procedures outlined here must *always and without exception,* carried out on every occasion. All Crystal Dreaming practitioners are certified and will have been taught by myself or one of my authorised teachers.

Why you are working with crystals

As you have been drawn to work with crystals in this lifetime, there is little doubt that you have worked with them in the past in other incarnations. The more you work with them the more your past life memory will be recalled. You will receive ideas in dreams, meditations and through intuition as you actually place crystals on clients. Be open to this.

The key to successful healings

The key to all successful healings is your intention, your focus, your will to heal based on unconditional love for the person with which you are working and the beings you encounter. In this state you may be surprised to observe miracles happening during and after your sessions. It is *vital* in the Crystal Dreaming process that you do not suggest or use leading questions during your clients journey. Your voice and confident, reassuring tone can affect your client profoundly

ALWAYS ask open ended questions, *do not lead your client.*

Personal cleansing prior to a session

You are responsible as the healer for the well-being of every person that comes to you in trust for a healing. Take that trust seriously and observe the following procedures.

Whenever you are healing, give yourself time prior to the session to be still. Sit or stand in the centre of the space where you will be working, become aware of the column of light over your head. It stretches up, through the clouds and into space, returning to the Source of all light, the source of all love.

Open the crown chakra and breathe in light through your crown allowing it to wash through your body. Open a valve just below the ball of each foot and release any excess energy there as you breathe out. Then take the light down to your power centre (Hara), located just below the navel in the centre of your body and there build a star. Push light out in every direction and add to it with each breath, allowing it to grow, dissolving any negative thoughts or feelings, pushing them outwards to be released and transmuted into light.

Allow the light to fill your body and then expand and fill your aura, an egg or sphere of light that surrounds you, pushing out or dissolving any negative thoughts or feelings.

Then project a ray of pink from your own heart projecting feelings based on unconditional love for all things. Allow that to spread out from your heart.

As it expands it pushes out or dissolves all energies not totally aligned with unconditional love and fills the egg of light you are standing in.

Then project a violet/white light from the third eye which expands and fills the egg pushing out or dissolving all energies not totally aligned with light. Allow this sphere to reach a little beyond the pink sphere you have already created.

When your personal egg/sphere is complete, create a violet flame which licks your body and the outside of your egg, leaving a violet hue. Then place a sparkling gold protective criss-cross mesh on the outside of the egg and a platinum mesh on top of that, you may affirm that this mesh will only let love and light in and will repel all other thought forms. You may then say out loud

"I am light, I am love, I am protected"

You are now cleansed, protected and in a fit state to share healing energy with others. Repeat this process after every session if required or at any other time that you feel uncomfortable. As a Crystal Dreaming practitioner, whether you are healing or not, you should practice this technique every day morning and night.

Further self protection

Always cleanse and protect yourself prior to every healing session and *after* every healing session. In addition to your normal practice you may rub pure sandalwood oil on every chakra or the nape of the neck, solar plexus and rear base chakras. Lapis may be worn around the neck, a gold crucifix worn on the nape of the neck, drops of mountain penny royal diluted and swallowed before and after sessions and anything else that makes you *feel* protected.

Your best protection is the unconditional love that surrounds you and your trust that the Universe will not present you with anything you can not deal with. As you become more powerful as a healer you will need less three dimensional support, but at the beginning use anything that makes you feel comfortable.

Shamanic breathing

Place your tongue against the hard palette inside your mouth. Now breathing in deeply through the nose, draw in light from the crown with each breath pushing the lower stomach out as you breathe in. Fill your being with light, allowing any stale energy to exit via the chakras in the feet.

Release the tongue and breathe out through the mouth pulling the stomach in, consciously expelling any stale energy and old air from the lungs. Continue until you feel light and refreshed.

You may use the 'plunging' technique described later. You may also find it useful to breathe in over a set period, hold the breath for the same length of time and then exhale for the same length of time eg. breathe in for 6 seconds, hold for 6 seconds, exhale for 6 seconds then hold for 6 seconds and repeat the cycle.

Clearing the space prior to your session

As you make the following invocation, you will visualise light surrounding you, and also entering your crown. You will project a ray of pink from your own heart projecting unconditional love for all things. Allow that to spread out from your heart, forming a pink sphere that as it expands into your healing space. It pushes out or dissolves all energies not totally aligned with unconditional love. It covers the whole area that you will be working in that day eg. the whole house or healing centre.

You may then project a violet/white light from the third eye which expands and fills the space pushing out or dissolving all energies not totally aligned with light. Allow this sphere to reach a little beyond the pink sphere you have already created. As you do this, you will also say clearly, out loud:

"Light! Light! Light!
I call on the Light of the Source
I call on the Light of my own Higher Self
I call on the Light of my own Mastery.
I call on the beings who love me unconditionally."

You may also call on and name any loving Ascended being with whom you work provided they love you unconditionally.

If you wish you may burn good quality sandalwood or frankincense incense before and after each session.

Grounding yourself

After cleansing the space you may need to ground yourself. You may create roots extending from the foot chakras, a point in the centre of the foot just below the ball of the foot. Allow these roots to penetrate deeply into Mother Earth, at least one metre. If you are very sensitive to crystals I recommend wearing or carrying grounding stones whilst healing (eg Iron Tiger, hematite or red jasper).

When you should not heal

It is totally inappropriate for you to enter a healing session if for any reason you are in an emotional state or depressed. Should this situation arise, cancel the session and seek a healer yourself.

A healer should be centred, happy, alert, physically fit and ready to share unconditional love with every client. NEVER attempt a healing if you are not in a fit state to do so, you will do more harm than good to both yourself and the client. NEVER attempt a healing if you are under the influence of alcohol or drugs.

A healer's lifestyle

It is inappropriate for a healer to be addicted to anything. Anyone in this state is disempowering themselves by not exerting their own will power over their own life situation.

These days many of your clients will be non-smokers, for them it may be unpleasant to be close to someone who emanates a smell of tobacco. If you are a smoker consider breaking the habit. Smoking marijuana opens up your Aura making you vulnerable to psychic attack. An unnecessary hindrance for a Crystal Dreaming practitioner.

Meat eating lowers your vibration as a channel, consider reducing or stopping your consumption of meat. Most people do not need it, those who do need it, eat it in moderation.

Exercise and meditation will help keep you fit, alert and centred. A healer who is exerting their own will power in relation to their own life will be able to achieve remarkable results.

Conclusion

Yourself, your crystals and the space you will be working in are cleansed, you are now ready to set up your Crystal Dreaming mandala.

Chapter 7
The process begins

Crystal Dreaming™ is not a form of counselling

In all aspects of Crystal Dreaming, you should not probe too deeply or get caught up in analysing and processing emotion. We are not creating a counselling situation, we are working on release and repair on a spiritual level. Do not analyse your clients experiences or explain them to them. They are what they are and they are easily understood. Never lead your client.

Entering the world of Crystal Dreaming and embarking with work in the spiritual plane, it is important to understand that in any situation, anywhere, at any time, no being has power over you or your client unless you allow it. You will in the course of your work encounter misguided beings who are under the illusion that they can exert power over others. Remember, you are a Divine being of light with complete free-will, you are powerful and unique. *Nothing has power over you unless you allow it.*

As Divine and powerful multidimensional beings, what we will, will come to pass. Think and express yourself carefully and at all times be particularly aware of thoughts or desires that are verbalised during a session. *Think before you speak*, your invocations have great power. Indeed you will discover that invocations made by your client whilst in an altered state also have great power, the results usually manifesting instantly.

We will now walk through the Crystal Dreaming process in a typical and "easy" session. In subsequent chapters I will guide you through the more challenging situations you may encounter.

The power of affirmations in your sacred space

You have created a sacred space for your client, combined with the altered state your client will access, you have a powerful situation in which you can create magical transformations for your client through affirmations. In Crystal Dreaming we use affirmations a great deal.

There are several key phrases which your client should say whenever possible, before every affirmation as these phrases increase the power of any affirmation. These key phrases are:

"Of my own free will..."

Your client is stating out loud that they are not being coerced into making this affirmation.

"Across time and space..."

This affirmation covers all times and planes of existence.

"In full consciousness..."

Your client is not asleep, dreaming, or under the influence of mind altering drugs or hypnosis.

"As the Universe is my witness..."

Your client is calling on the whole of creation to witness and support their choice.

Another important addition to any affirmation is the word:

"NOW."

This focuses energies, inter-dimensional beings and spirit beings who exist in other realities, in other times or in a never ending now, to this point in time and space here on Earth.

It is not always possible to include these conditions if you are thinking fast and have to move quickly, or if your client is having difficulty speaking. However they add power and clarity to any affirmation so use them whenever you can.

Greeting your client

The area is cleared, sealed and protected, you are fit, alert, cleansed and your crystal mandala is laid out. You are now ready to start a session. Be warm, friendly and open with all clients. Listen to what they have to say. Explain a little about the session, but not too much, you do not want to suggest what their experience might be. It is a distraction to talk a great deal prior to a session, you do not need to. Your client interview will last about five minutes.

Trauma

Ask your client have they experienced any major trauma in their lives. Whether it be a car or skiing accident, childhood abuse or any other form of trauma it is useful for you to know. It may come up in the session, particularly if it opened your client (through pain or fear) to any form of spirit attachment, which is common.

It is important for both your well-being and your efficiency that you practice compassionate detachment from your client. You cannot get involved with your client's trauma. You cannot empathise with them. You will witness a great deal of trauma release and recall in your practice and it is important that it does not affect you. One way of looking at it which may help you is to understand that on the highest level, there are no victims only volunteers.

Nausea prior to a healing

You are interested to know how your client feels prior to a session. If a person feels nauseous or sick on entering the space you have prepared, or has had a restless night prior to the healing, it is often an indication that there is some form of negative energy or an entity with your client. Existing in a fear based reality, the entity feels uncomfortable in the cleansed space or approaching it.

Some questions on greeting your client:

"How do you feel?"

"How was your journey here?"

"How did you sleep last night?"

"Why have you come to see me?"

"Have you been through any major trauma in your life?"

Preparing your client

Ask your client to lie down on their back in the mandala you have already prepared. Be sure they keep their eyes open until you are ready to start the session. If you turn your back on your client to close curtains and they close their eyes, some may slip into an unguided altered state immediately as they are lying in your crystal mandala.

When you are ready, they will be lying with their *head pointing towards magnetic north*, arms by their side palms up. You will tell them when you are about to place crystals on their body. You may ask them to repeat after you...

"I promise to speak with you at all times during the session.

I promise to return to my physical body at the end of this journey when you call me back.

I authorise you to intercede on my behalf should it become necessary."

If your client is not talking to you, you cannot effectively monitor their progress and they will also forget what is happening if they do not verbalise their experience. It can sometimes be difficult for people to return from the blissful place to which they travel, a binding promise which they make can help you call them back. You may also need to act quickly in a session without explaining why.

Ask the client to then shut their eyes and focus on their breathing. Your client will remain fully clothed and you may even cover them if it is cool. Crystal energy will easily penetrate clothing and covers. There is no need to touch your client during any Crystal Dreaming session.

Entering an altered state

Observe the client as they lie down. Those who are more sensitive will start to shift consciousness immediately, as soon as their head touches the pillow and they enter the powerful crystal mandala you have already prepared. You will need to *keep them talking*, and you may even need to remove some of the crystals around the crown if they enter a deep state too quickly or they will rapidly lose awareness of this reality and your directions.

The most obvious sign of a shift in consciousness is a rapid fluttering of the eyelids and eyes. It is totally involuntary and may become quite pronounced and the client may need reassurance that it is quite normal. *Do not tell them they are moving into an altered state* at this or any other time during the healing. Keep talking and gently eliciting a response as you guide them through the following Crystal Dreaming process.

You may find yourself also entering an altered state as the client does, *resist this*. It is important that you are totally grounded during your session, and not travelling with the client. Do not observe them through clairvoyance, as this can interfere with their experience. You may find yourself leading them by "helping" them, suggesting what they might experience based on your perceptions. If you need to stay grounded during a session wear a hematite anklet or bracelet.

Travelling with the client is an advanced technique which I teach to experienced practitioners on request. Do not attempt it without training, it is dangerous as you are placing yourself in a vulnerable position.

Hematite grounding

If you feel your client may need extra grounding (which would be unusual) you may place around the body and close to it, an oval of small hematite tumblers, half a dozen is enough. These stones pin part of their consciousness here in this reality. If your client does not need further grounding you can leave the tumblers either side of the feet during the session or remove them.

For a "spaced out" client

If you perceive the client to be very ungrounded, (a rare occurrence) place two large tumblers of black obsidian, black tourmaline, hematite or iron tiger one below the heel of each foot. You may also place tumblers on each hip joint and under each knee. A grounding ball can also be useful to give a client to hold after a session (eg. an iron tiger ball or egg).

Crystals in hands, ball behind neck

Place a channelling, Dow or spirit quartz crystal in the palm of each hand, point towards the head. Ensure the purple fluorite ball is sitting comfortably in the hollow at the base of the skull at the back of your client's neck.

Invocation

At this point you should centre yourself, open your heart chakra and send out love as you call on your own and your client's spiritual team, naming the client you will say out loud:

> *"I call on _____'s Higher Self. I call on _____ 's spiritual guides, teachers and friends. Please be with us today. Please share with us your healing energies and protection.*
>
> *I call on my own Higher Self. I call on my own Mastery. I call on my Spiritual guides, teachers and friends. I call on the beings who love us unconditionally. Please be with us today. Please share with us your healing energies and protection. I ask in full faith. So be it."*

Cleansing

Do not use the same process of cleansing on your client as you did on yourself. Suggest the client listen to the sound of their own breath, gently breathing in and out bringing themselves to this moment. When the client is relaxed and still, ask them to "become aware" of a column of light over their head. *Do not use the words "imagine" or "visualise."*

> *"Become aware of a column of light above your head. It stretches up through the clouds, into the stars and beyond, back to the Source of all light, the source of all love. It is uninterrupted Divine energy, a vibrant golden white light. It pours down on your head and shoulders and follows you everywhere, like a spotlight. (Pause).*
>
> *Now notice a white flower with many petals on top of your head. Allow the flower to open as if to the morning sun. As it opens, gently breathe light in through the flower from the column above your head into your body. (Pause).*
>
> *As you breathe light in through the flower allow it to pick up any negative thoughts or feelings and take them down towards the feet. Open a tap or valve in the centre of each foot just below the ball of each foot. As you breathe out allow the old energy out, returning to Mother Earth. With each breath draw more light into your body from the column above, sparkling and tingling, gently caressing and filling your body with light. As you breath out release any excess energy through the open valves in your feet."*

Plunging

> *"Create a disk of light as wide as your body hovering above the*

top of your head. Fill the disk with light from the column above. When it is full and bright, take a deep breath in and on the out breath plunge the disk down through your body like a coffee plunger."

Repeat this process three times, plunging emerald green, royal blue and iridescent violet discs one after the other. Ensure the foot chakras are open prior to plunging. Each plunge of colour cleanses and lifts the vibration of your client, particularly the violet.

Conclusion

Your client is now in a still place and ready to move deeper into the process.

Chapter 8
Scanning

Full body X-Ray

Your client is in a relaxed and still place, next they will scan their body from above. Ask if they notice anything unusual or uncomfortable as they scan their body. Ask them what they *"perceive"* rather than "see."

> *"Look down on your body from above, as if you have CAT scan or X-ray eyes. Using all your senses, looking, feeling, sensing, probing, scan the energy inside and around your body, starting above the head and working all the way down to below the feet. As you work your way down through your body tell me if you notice anything unusual or uncomfortable."*

They may perceive nothing, they may perceive a great deal. Fortunately, most people perceive conditions in the etheric, emotional or physical bodies in graphic clear pictures, or feelings which translate into pictures. If they say they can't "see" anything suggest they use their feelings. These feelings will normally translate quickly clear impressions or stories, with your encouragement.

Do not let your client undermine the process by telling you they can't "see" anything. They are expecting a movie, when in fact they can perceive a great deal very clearly through their emotions and sensations in their body. They may feel something heavy on their chest but not see anything. Ask them what it is made of, what environment they are in. The information is there, all they have to do, with your patient help, is tap into it.

Feelings, when explored usually translate into a clearly understandable story. Most clients, fortunately do see quite well.

Your client may perceive dense dark energy in certain parts of their body, it may appear as red, grey, dark or muddy. Dark or red energy around the root chakra and reproductive organs may indicate childhood sexual abuse. Allow the client to discover this, do not lead them.

They may perceive black dots of energy around the head, limbs may be distorted, missing or frozen. They may also notice negative energy in the form of dark balls or clouds on, around or outside the body.

They may see a dagger or spear in their body, a noose around their neck or chains around their feet. This kind of blockage generally relates to past life trauma or a traumatic past life death. They may notice a crystal embedded in a chakra.

They may even notice someone standing close to them.

Scan the whole body from head to toe, making a note of each blockage as the client comes to it. Then return to the top start again and clear each blockage as you come to it.

Spirit attachment

One of the most common form of negative energy blockage that shows up in the scan is spirit attachment. They may appear as a person standing next to the client in the scan. These beings are usually Earthbound spirits, dead people who at the moment of death became confused or for other reasons refused their opportunity to transit home to light and unity consciousness.

Sometimes sentient beings such as Earthbound spirits appear as dark solid balls of energy that move away from the light that your client draws in, as it is uncomfortable for them. They may also try and distract your client by creating feelings of nausea, a full bladder or pain that moves around the body. Always suggest your client visit the toilet before a session for this reason. You can then presume that any full bladder sensation is an illusion created by an entity to stop the session. Your client can say out loud talking to the energy;

> *"I am aware of your presence, what do you want? Show yourself to me now. Don't be afraid, I promise not to hurt you."*

Most earthbound spirits are happy to return home to light without too much fuss. They may have something to say to your client and likewise your client may wish to thank them for their help, for they most likely will have responded to your clients request for help during some trauma in their past. They do not always realise they are dead and will be stuck in the year that they died. Your client may ask:

> *"What year is it? Do you realise you are dead?"*

The confused spirit may then need a bit of counselling:

> *"It is now (name the year you are in). Your body is long gone. There is a much nicer place to go to than staying here with me. Please let me help you."*

When they are ready to leave of their own free will the easiest way of assisting an Earthbound spirit is for your client to call on the Earthbound spirit's own spirit guides to help three times out loud.

> *"I call on this person's spirit guides, I call on this person's spirit guides, I call on this person's spirit guides.*
>
> *Please come close to us and help this person journey home to light and find peace. Now."*

Your client will then perceive lights, beings, people, guides or angels approaching the attached spirit. They may need to reassure the spirit that it's OK for them to leave with the beings who have come to help.

If the attached spirit is a child call on their angels as their guides may appear frightening to them as they will not know them.

If the spirit has been attached for a long time then your client may get quite emotional as they leave, the attached spirit has been keeping them company and supporting them for years. After the session you will advise your client that this grieving process may go on for several days. This is normal and will dissipate, particularly if your client consciously nurtures themselves during this period.

Not all earthbound spirits are co-operative; we will deal with more challenging situations later in this book.

Indications that a person may have a spirit attachment

Always ask your client how they slept the night prior to a healing and how they felt on their way to the healing. Interrupted sleep and bad dreams are an indication that there may be a presence attached. Misgivings about attending the session or nausea on entering the space you have prepared are other clear indications that something may be amiss. Any violent body spasms when you lay on crystals or a blocked journey indicate probable attachment. Trust your intuition; you will very often know as soon as your client enters the room.

Benign Earthbound spirits

You may encounter an apparently benign spirit attached to your client by mutual consent given in a past life. They are not one of their guides as their love is conditional. These are often people who in a past lifetime made a binding agreement never to leave the person, ever. They could also be a deceased relative or friend who does not realise they are dead. Their presence, whilst being well motivated, will not help either your client, or the spirit itself, evolve. You will help them return to light using the technique above.

Proceeding with a Crystal Dreaming session will not be productive unless you can persuade any attached spirit to go home to light and accept the help of their spirit guides. Its presence will block your client's access to their own true higher guidance, the higher dimensions and their spiritual team.

Releasing blocked or negative energy

The client should now scan for a second time from above the head down, this time stopping at each area of discomfort in turn from the top down, unless something is urgently demanding their attention. Starting with the first area you may suggest:

"Draw light through the open flower on your crown, from the inexhaustible source above your head. Take it down through the middle of your body to the centre of your arm/throat/leg etc. From the centre with each out-breath gently push out thousands of pinpricks of light into the area of discomfort. Observe what happens."

Ask your client to tell you what happens without suggesting anything to them.

The way that the blockage responds to this technique tells you a great deal about it, so *do not lead the client* by suggesting that the light will break up or dissolve the energy blockage. They are to observe and tell you what happens. If it is just a temporary accumulation of negative energy the pinpricks will dissolve the energy completely. If this does not happen or if the energy starts to move around the body and cause more discomfort or pain, then one of the following techniques may be used to release it.

Cellular memory

It is possible as you dissolve energy with light that the client may have a spontaneous and graphic recall of the experience relating to the blockage. This can be an emotional experience.

If we are not able to deal with emotional trauma in the moment we experience it then our energy body holds the memory of the event in the cells of the part of our body that the trauma relates to. We store the experience to be released when we are strong enough to deal with it. We store all of our experiences in every cell of our body, particularly emotionally painful experiences that were too intense for us to deal with in the moment. This is called our cellular memory.

Whilst the initial recall from this or a past life may often appear as a physical trauma it will *always* relate to an *emotional* trauma. We experience all sorts of physical trauma over many lifetimes but it is the emotional trauma that really hurts us deeply and this is the trauma we hang on to. Our physical bodies are renewed as we reincarnate, our emotional bodies continue to grow indefinitely and so will store emotional trauma indefinitely until the opportunity to release it occurs.

Past life trauma

Past life trauma is common and often appears in the scan. It can present spontaneously for release at any time. It will appear as it happened physically and it will usually relate to a past life death. During the scan if your client perceives a dagger in their chest or a noose around their neck chances are that when they command their body to release the cellular memory they will move into a recall of a traumatic past life death.

Your client may well start feeling intense emotion that may include anger, fear, or deep sadness, before they perceive any images or clear recall of the incident. They will need reassurance that it will benefit their lives enormously if they persevere and release it. If the trauma is major then the scene may be revealed a little at a time, ask them to say out loud:

"I give myself permission to remember exactly what happened to me; body show me now."

Remember always, it is the emotional not the physical trauma you are dealing with. The key is to change the way your client *feels* about the experience in the past, which affects their state of being now. If past life trauma is not released it may lead to a repeat of the trauma in this life or if unresolved may lead to serious illness related to the part of the body in which the trauma is held.

There may be layers of similar trauma from a series of lifetimes in the same part of the body. Often trauma that is being recreated in the present leads to this revelation. Do not presume that as you have released one trauma it has all cleared, check the area again on a subsequent scan.

To assist with the healing process your body may help by drawing attention to the trauma by experiencing repeated minor injuries to the part of the body in which the trauma is held. For example, if a client mentions they have repeated, inexplicable injuries and minor accidents that relate to their forearm, then you can expect the scan to reveal a trauma held in the forearm. Remember *do not lead your client,* let them discover it for themselves. See the case study "Scarred arms" at the rear of this book.

The important thing for you as a therapist is to establish what happened, why it happened and who was responsible. With this knowledge you can then move into the release process. Recall of the trauma can be released with the following simple command. Ask your client to say out loud:

"Body I command you take me to the moment this happened."

Or

"Body I command you release the cellular memory I am holding here, into full consciousness now. Show me exactly what happened. Now."

Wait and if necessary repeat the affirmation with the free will, time space, witness and fully conscious prefixes advised earlier. Your client's body may need reassurance that the painful memory it is about to release can be dealt with. Ask them to say out loud:

"I dissolve any agreements I have made with myself for my own protection."

Or

"I dissolve any agreements I have made with any other being regarding remembering what happened to me. Body I command you take me to the moment this started. Now."

These affirmations are particularly relevant in recalling present life childhood sexual abuse or a past life death through sacrifice or torture. Your client may have promised themselves they would never use their innate healing and psychic powers ever again eg. when being tortured and burned at the stake as a witch.

It is quite OK that your client re-experience the trauma, it will not last long. The intensity of the experience will also help override any doubts that might creep in after the session about the authenticity of their experience during the session.

Forgiveness

The key to any release of this nature is forgiveness. In fact if you are in doubt about any situation that arises in any session then ask yourself, how can I apply forgiveness to this situation? The answer will often lead you to a solution. By forgiving others who may have harmed them, forgiving themselves if they have harmed others or been angry with themselves for their choices, your client can release the trauma, once and for all.

Whatever memory surfaces during this process it is important that your client forgive themselves or others and acknowledge that the experience was their choice and was perfect. They have learnt a great deal from it and no longer need to hold on to it. Addressing the person who killed them they can say:

"Across Time and Space I call on the beings responsible for my death/torture/humiliation, etc. Please stand before me now."

They will arrive quickly, be sure they are there and that your client perceives them before you continue. Ask your client to say out loud:

"I forgive you, I forgive you, I forgive you. With all my heart I freely forgive you.

In forgiving you I release you from this trauma, as I release myself, to find joy, peace, happiness and freedom. Go in peace, thank you.

We are no longer bound by this trauma. You are released, go in peace."

They will normally bow graciously and leave, whether they are being forgiven or giving forgiveness. To complete the process, if they still feel traumatised, your client might say, as they breathe light and unconditional love into the area where the trauma was held:

> *"I surrender to the perfection of this death.*
>
> *Everything is perfect, all my choices are perfect. My choice to experience this event has served me well and I have learnt a great deal from it and do not need to repeat it. I forgive anyone who has harmed me.*
>
> *It was OK to feel the way I did when I had this experience, but I choose now to leave it in the past where it belongs. I leave all feelings of guilt/despair/grief etc in the past where they belong. This experience now ceases to have any power over me as I release it to be transmuted into light, for the divine highest good of all."*

Soul retrieval

Occasionally a client will experience an extreme past life trauma where after the usual release process they witness themselves as being stuck or Earthbound. In this case the soul has fragmented and left part of itself behind.

Integrating and absorbing that part of the client during the session may seem the obvious way to go and for the experienced practitioner this is an option. However Earthbound spirits and entities can be tricky and they may wish to confuse your client.

The foolproof way of resolving this is to have that part of themselves returned to unity consciousness with help from their team.

> *"I call upon the beings that love me unconditionally (x3). Please be here now and assist me in releasing this fragmented part of myself to be absorbed into oneness and bliss. Please return this fragmented part of my being to unity consciousness so that I may become integrated, whole and complete, on the highest level. Now."*

Those who will not accept forgiveness

If the beings who your clients has called on will not forgive or accept forgiveness, or if they express anger then there is a good chance they are Earthbound and do not realise that they are dead. Suggest your client ask them the key questions covered earlier:

> *"What year is it? Do you realise you are dead?"*

Follow the procedures for helping Earthbound spirits outlined earlier.

Present life trauma

At this point, if the blockage was created in this life then your client will relive a trauma probably from childhood. This memory when it surfaces may be both shocking and painful for your client to deal with, they will probably have the whole scene replayed into their consciousness. Parts of the scene may be unclear at first (eg. the faces of the perpetrators). In which case your client needs to reassure their body that they are ready to face the truth, all will then gradually be revealed usually over several replays.

Any recall will relate to the emotional rather than the physical trauma experienced, although as mentioned earlier the physical location of the trauma is where you will start to unlock the memory by commanding the body to release it.

At this point your client may be feeling a mixture of shame, guilt, deep sadness or anger. They will need reassurance again that it is okay, now is the time, they can deal with the issue once and for all. We are not dealing with a figment of their imagination. Remind them, if necessary, that you did not programme them, make suggestions or probe in any way for this revelation, it came from their own consciousness in response to an open ended affirmation. Explain that the best way to lay this matter to rest is to forgive the perpetrators of any injury inflicted on them.

This might seem like a tall order at first, but you must help your client understand that the only way to release this incident is to do so with love. Unconscious burning anger or shame continues a connection with both the incident and the perpetrators which creates negative emotions and blockages in other areas of your life. When your client is ready to deal with it you should call on the spirit of the perpetrator. Even if the perpetrator is still alive you should still call on their spirit, it will come.

Your client has nothing to fear with this interaction. What will probably happen without you suggesting anything is that the spirit will approach and humbly apologise for their actions. It is appropriate that you instruct them through your client to kneel in front of your client and beg forgiveness.

It is probably timely, and will no doubt help the confused individual who perpetrated the incident, but you are not doing this particularly for them, it is your client who will benefit from this action and they may need reminding of this. Forgiveness must come from the heart, it is enough for your client to state out loud:

> "*I forgive you, I forgive you, I forgive you. With all my heart I forgive you. In forgiving you I release you from this trauma, as I release myself to find joy, peace happiness and freedom. Go in peace,*

thank you. We are both (all) now released from this trauma, it no longer binds us."

This incident has now ceased to have any hold over your client, they are free of its influence.

In the unlikely event that the perpetrator does not beg forgiveness of their own accord, you are dealing with an earthbound spirit. You may choose to explain that the perpetrator's selfish actions have caused unnecessary pain and suffering. Whatever transpires, your client must forgive them regardless of their behaviour, you will then offer to assist the earthbound spirit to transit. Even if you do end up with a lost soul who has difficulty dealing with the whole procedure the important thing is that your client forgive and so release the cellular memory and break the energetic attachment to the perpetrator once and for all.

You should continue the session and make contact with the clients team when you do so, ask them to fill your client with love, light and healing energy and carry out any repair work on your clients energy bodies. Your client will finish the session in a blissful but emotionally drained state and may be tired afterwards.

Childhood sexual abuse

Recall of childhood sexual abuse may arise at any time during the scan or later in the session. As a method of defence and self preservation the body will store the memory until an appropriate opportunity presents to release it. It is not uncommon for mature women to suddenly remember an incident of childhood sexual abuse which has been stored as an energy blockage since the incident, the memory being too traumatic to deal with until this moment in your session. It may show up as red energy over the root chakra during your initial scan.

It is *vital* that the healer continue to reassure the client that it is OK to let it go, it will be released once and for all. Do not stop the session and comfort your client. In fact *you must never touch your client at any time*. You must remain detached from their trauma release.

Continue, gently reassuring, without probing too deeply. As a therapist, you do not need to know too much detail about this type of trauma. It is appropriate to call on the spirit of anyone who has caused your client to suffer, whether they are alive or dead and to give them the opportunity to ask for forgiveness. Whatever happens, it is essential your client forgive any hurt, as the anger and fear associated with the incident creates an energetic tie to the perpetrator which will be an ongoing drain on your client's energy. Having called on the perpetrator(s) your client will say out loud:

"I forgive you, I forgive you, I forgive you. With all my heart I freely forgive you. I forgive you for abusing my trust, I forgive your selfishness and lack of consideration for my well-being. In forgiving you I release you from this trauma, as I release myself, to find joy, peace, happiness and freedom. Go in peace, this trauma no longer binds us, we are both released from it."

Until they surrender to the perfection of their experience and release the fear based emotions attached to it, their experience will continue to have power over them. Holding on to the trauma through lack of forgiveness will prevent your session from continuing into unconditional love. This is most challenging with present life trauma.

These intense emotions will subside surprisingly quickly and in the post trauma state, your client can do some profound repair work on the heart chakra:

"Drawing light in through the crown from the inexhaustible source above your head, take it through the heart centre mixing it with unconditional love, rebuilding and repairing the heart, opening a beautiful pink flower there."

The chakra can be made whole again and repaired permanently. Further repair work may be carried out later in the session by the clients own team.

A word of caution for male healers

No matter how emotional your clients gets, *do not touch their body* to comfort them. Be tactful and restrained, you do not need a great deal of information, have an understanding of the relationships with those involved and focus on encouraging the release through forgiveness and follow up with repair work.

Energy vampires

Occasionally, your client may discover strands of energy running away from their body or chakras, they are to see where they lead. They may discover that someone they have met is drawing energy from them without their conscious permission. This is less common than you might expect.

Find out why this is happening and tell the person that they no longer have permission to do this and they must stop. It may be interesting for your client to understand more about how this started. In which case you could suggest they say the following:

"Body, show me the moment this started."

When your client is ready they may cut the chords leading to that person with a laser, sword or scissors and ensure the point of contact is thoroughly cleansed with light drawn in through the body from above the crown. As they cut the chords they can see that the chords burn away with light like a fuse disintegrating as it leaves their body.

ET Implants

Another blockage can become apparent at this time. It is immediately obvious to the client that it is not a part of their natural energy systems. These blockages appear to the client as tiny dots, wires or bars of sometimes intense discomfort. They can appear anywhere in the body but often appear around the nasal and sinus area, the ears, throat and temples. They may sometimes appear as wires running down the body. These require some explanation.

Etheric as well as physical abductions of humans by extraterrestrials and interdimensionals, has been going on for many years. These misguided beings have been seeking mostly to observe and occasionally manipulate our species for their own ends. The implants affect our etheric bodies, even though most of the time there is no particular malice at work. In fact many ETs that interfere with us have no emotions at all.

The beings who place the implants are not positive loving beings and never ask permission to either abduct or place implants in humans. If implants have been placed without your clients conscious permission they have no right to be there and should be removed.

Do not tell the client about the nature of this type of blockage when they discover it, they will realise what it is later in the session. If they ask, you may refer to it as an energy blockage.

How to remove implants

The easiest way to remove the implants is to call on the beings who placed them there to step forward and show themselves.

> *"Whoever placed this here, step forward and show yourself to me now."*

The client will normally perceive an ET, often a small grey one. They will then explain to it that they have no right to leave the implants in their body, without their conscious permission and they must remove them, now.

If no one steps forward you may ask the client to command their body to show them the moment this started or it was placed here.

> *"Body show me the moment this was placed here, take me there now."*

Your client may have a sudden recall of a bizarre dream in which they were abducted by aliens. It was not a dream, their etheric body was removed and tampered without their conscious permission.

If you encounter resistance with the being you encounter, go up the chain of command. Ask to see the ETs supervisor and keep going until you find one that understands this is a free will zone and they cannot implant people without their conscious permission. Be courteous and polite at all times.

> *"You must remove this now, I no longer need it and you do not have my permission to leave this here. Thank you for allowing me to look after it for you, I no longer need it. Please remove it now and go in peace."*

If there is resistance...

> *"You know this is a free will zone and you may not leave it here without my consent. You no longer have my consent, please remove it now. Thank you."*

Once it is removed have your client remind the ETs they cannot come back without their conscious written permission.

> *"Thank you for removing it, go in peace. You may not return without my conscious written permission."*

Then have the client massage the area with light and unconditional love and ensure it feels comfortable before you move on.

If you are unable to negotiate a removal, which would be most unusual, you may assist your client to remove them.

Removing these implants may be painful and may even cause a slight bleeding, so warn the client that they may experience some discomfort. They are best removed by both you and the client working together using your will-power to push or pull them out of the nearest body opening.

> *"Push the implant outwards by drawing in light from above your head and gently pushing the object out of the neared body opening (ear/nose/throat/eyes etc)."*

Generally you will find them in the ears, nose, throat and temples and they can be removed if you persevere. Your client will see and feel them leave their body and you may feel the implant drop into your hand if you are holding it the exit point. Dispose of it by throwing it into a ball of vibrant green or violet light. Kunzite may also assist with dissolving implants.

Do not try and break them up with light. They can replicate, multiply and disperse themselves around the body.

Misguided ETs

You may encounter ETs with a client, usually prior to their connection with their guides. Ask for a description with open ended questions. There are many, some of the most commonly encountered are:

Greys

These are small, slim bluey-grey with large dark almond shaped eyes, they do not emit light and love and will not be focused on your client's Divine highest good. They have no sense of humour and are not positive beings. They are usually connected with implants. After ensuring your client is free of implants using techniques outlined earlier, they will ask the ET to leave:

"You must leave me now, our agreement is complete, you no longer have my permission be here. Thank you for teaching me my limitations go in peace. You are released."

If there is resistance...

"You know this is a free will zone and you may not stay here without my consent. You no longer have my consent, please leave now. Thank you."

If you have any challenges with uncooperative ETs just demand to speak with their supervisor and keep going up the chain of command until you find a being that understands the truth of universal law and free will.

Extraterrestrial abduction

Occasionally in a session a person will have a graphic recall of an ET abduction. As the good ones do not abduct humans, you are dealing with misguided and heartless beings, probably Greys. If it feels right the client can re-run the incident and at the time when they feel most vulnerable or fearful make the following affirmation:

"I am a free spirit. You have no power over me, you never have had any power over me nor will you ever have any power over me. Across Time and Space, as the Universe is my witness, I dissolve all ties and agreements I may have made with you. I am a being of light, I am a being of love, I am inviolate, I am that I am, I am a free Spirit! So be it.

I now command all implants, crystals or any other devices placed in any of my bodies without my conscious written permission be removed immediately."

Their surprised abductors will release them and they will be returned to Earth. Occasionally you may have to move up the chain of command but the implants will be removed eventually.

Orions

Negative Orions have a Darth Vader like appearance and will attempt to intimidate you and your client. They are warriors whose interest lies in power over rather than power with. Neither being believe we are a particularly intelligent species, which is not surprising considering the way we are treating our planet. They may be removed by reminding them they have no right to be here under universal law, you may also appeal to their vanity.

After finding out how they came to be there and the nature of their agreement, your client should make the following affirmation:

"Thank you for helping me and coming when I asked you to. Our agreement is now complete. I have learnt all I need to know about... (fear etc) you no longer have my permission to be here. Please leave me now and go in peace, you know you cannot stay without my conscious written permission. I am a sovereign being of light, I reclaim my sovereignty, I reclaim my power, I reclaim my freedom. Go in peace. Now!"

Be firm and clear and do not take no for an answer. You may also offer any Orion a challenge to step into the light. There are also positive, evolved Orions who appear dressed in dark brown monk like habits, you may call on them for assistance if you need to:

"I call on a positive Orion to join us and counsel their brother who has become confused."

Normally the two will have a dialogue and the dark Orion will leave.

It is preferable but not essential to guide any being home to light, the primary objective is to free your client from its influence and ensure it does not have permission to return:

"You may not return without my conscious written permission."

Reptoids

You may also encounter another species of being who are usually inter-dimensional rather than extraterrestrial. These reptile-like part humanoid creatures will create a sense of deep fear and panic when your client becomes aware of their presence. The most common form of reptoid you will encounter is not ET, rather they are the ancient inhabitants of this planet existing in a slightly higher dimensional reality close to us.

When you attempt to interact with them you may well receive an earful of abuse. Their grasp of our beautiful language seems to focus on profanities and four letter words. Certainly they will instil fear into your client. Occasionally you may encounter another species of inter-dimensional/ET reptoid who are smarter and more articulate than their Earthbound cousins.

Either way, your aim is to help them understand that they have no business with your client and they must leave. It is essential that your client does not collapse into fear as this is the energy that they feed off. They will leave if you are persistent, as they need your client's permission to stay. Remember if you believe they will leave, so will your client. Do not doubt it.

For those who do not meet their guides

Not everyone meets their guides on their first journey. Sometimes there is just too much clearing for one session and the client has to focus solely on clearing. Some clients will block the meeting through not allowing or constantly questioning, analysing or even denying what is happening. Sometimes it is just not appropriate to meet them at that time.

For many clients the experience of feeling truly relaxed and at peace is enough, connecting with animals and nature with love. Always people benefit from the experience. Do not lead, or control through suggestion, this part of the journey.

Implanted crystals

If your client perceives crystals inside their body, anywhere, particularly in their chakras, this may not be a good thing. Crystals may have been implanted by a sorcerer or high priestess from a past life, ETs or interdimensionals. Their purpose will be to limit your clients power, "protect" them, drain energy or monitor them. The following affirmation you can also apply where there is any other form of suspected implant:

"Whoever placed this here, show yourself to me. Now!"

Your client will quickly perceive the being who placed the crystal in their body. You may discover more about their relationship, how the crystal came to be there and what its purpose is:

"What is our relationship? Why did you place this here?"

If it is not for their Divine highest good or given in unconditional love then your client may say something like...

"Thank you for leaving it there, it has served me well. I have learnt a great deal from looking after it, but I no longer need it. You can remove it now, it has been an honour looking after it for you."

Your client should be polite and patient, they are normally removed easily.

Stubborn entities

There are other beings that will avoid the light your client pushes into them when they appear as energy blockages or negative energy. They will move away as your client focuses light on them, the light may even appear to hurt them. This behaviour indicates a self aware entity or intelligent being.

Most negative energy blockages will dissolve in reasonable time by channelling pinpricks of light into them, however an entity will resist the process by avoiding light and causing the client to feel pain or nausea. It will move around the body to avoid the light being channelled towards it. Your client may end up having a series of severe stabbing pains that move as you attempt to deal with them. These types of entity may appear as people, beings or energy that has form and intelligence. Your client may say the following:

"I am aware of your presence, show yourself to me and tell me what you want."

If there is no response or if the pain gets worse:

"Don't be afraid, I promise not to hurt you. I would like to thank you, I can help you. Step forward and tell me what you want."

It is important that you open a dialogue with any entity through your client so you can understand more about their relationship with your client and how you can help them. Remember when dealing with angry or aggressive entities that *anger is an indication that the entity you are dealing with is afraid.* Be compassionate, take your time, reassure, "request" rather than "command" and be patient.

You may also have your client command their body to release the cellular memory relating to the *moment* your client gave permission for it to be there. Knowledge is power, once you have opened a dialogue between client and entity you are in a position to find out more and devise strategies for helping the entity go home to light and find peace.

During this process the entity, because it is itself afraid, may attempt to create fear in your client and you, by threatening you both.

Dealing with fear

Should your client become fearful at any time during a session you should deal with it immediately. Fear is contagious, you must never allow yourself to become fearful because you become vulnerable if you do.

F E A R = False Expectations Appearing Real. Lead your client through the following affirmation, by saying it with them you will help yourself too.

"As the Universe is my witness, I choose to live in a fear free environment. I acknowledge my fear as a powerful friend that makes me alert and ready for action, and I thank it for serving me. However, fear does not control me.

I choose to centre myself in love and light, I choose to live love, be and share love. Nothing has power over me on this or any other plane. I am a sovereign being of light, my power is limitless. I choose peace, I choose joy, I choose love. Now."

Contracts and dissolving them

All attachments relate to contracts and agreements made by your client. They are rarely made in full consciousness or of your clients own free will. In order for any attachment, negative being or entity to remain in place it must have your clients permission. This is a universal truth and it applies to all beings, even though they may try and persuade your client otherwise. Your client could say:

"Thank you for your service, our agreement is now complete and is no longer binding. You are released from it. You are free now to go home to light, I can help you if you wish. Would you like that?"

Once the entity has agreed, (and it may need persuading) your client can create a column of light, like the one above their head, next to them and invite the being to step into it. Encourage the being to go up the column to return home to light. As the being ascends suggest that your client seal the column after the entity. Or they can call three times on the beings that love the entity unconditionally:

"I call on the beings that love this being unconditionally, I call on the beings that love this being unconditionally, I call on the beings that love this being unconditionally. Please come close to us now and help this being go home and find peace."

In the case of a simple entity this will be enough. They only need reassurance that their service is finished, that the light will not hurt them and they will leave. The entity may resist and become fearful of stepping into the light, or going with the beings of light that have come to help, it needs reassurance that it need not fear you or the light and that you are telling the truth, it will not be harmed. In many cases this will suffice, but if you encounter severe resistance, anger or threats, then you will need to use some of the techniques in the advanced section of this book, or stop the session and refer your client to a more experienced specialist.

During this process it is likely that your client will become aware of how this being was affecting their behaviour. They will probably also remember the time, place and circumstances which led them to make the agreement that allowed the entity to remain. In many cases your client will become emotional as the entity leaves. Reassure them that it is their choice to dissolve the agreement, and it is time to do so, as both parties are being held back by the agreement.

At this stage in the Crystal Dreaming process it is often the simpler entities that are revealed. The more intelligent beings may presume they can outsmart you and may remain hidden until later in the process. The process will reveal them in due course.

Counterfeit Masters

Your client may meet a well known Ascended Master or less well known Master. Our culture is not aware of all the Masters in service to this planet at this time. Use the appropriate protocols for checking their authenticity. If you are in the slightest doubt as to whether they love your client unconditionally, try the following affirmation asking your client to observe the being closely.

"I challenge your truth as a being of light!"

A true Master will be unaffected by this challenge, in their infinite patience and love for us they will happily answer with waves of unconditional love. A counterfeit Master will display momentary anger, their energy field will wobble for an instant. Light can be imitated, love cannot.

Suggest your client ask the master to show them their heart and project love at them. Elated giggles and a rush of energy may indicate a hoax, deep and profound emotion relating to infinite and powerful nature of love indicates the presence of a true Master.

Repeating the scan

Repeat the scanning process. For many people, most, sometimes all, of their first session can be spent in the scanning process. They may not get to the next stage of the process, this is OK. Clients may have spent many lifetimes experiencing trauma and picking up attachments. Your session may be their first opportunity in a long time to release them.

Remember your client will assist their healing process by filling any damaged area with light and unconditional love, instructing the cells to regenerate and repair. When you have reunited your client with their own team and checked their authenticity you will ask their team to check all your work. They can perceive things that you and your client may not be aware of.

Conclusion

Having scanned, cleansed and checked your clients energetic bodies and chakras and released any negative energy or simple entities, they are now in a suitable state to proceed with the main part of their Crystal Dreaming experience.

Chapter 9
The waterfall

When you are happy that your client's physical, etheric and emotional bodies are cleansed and nothing else is showing up in the scan, you are ready to start the Crystal Dreaming journey. The focus now is on creating a space where your client can meet their Higher Self, the beings that love them unconditionally, their guides, teachers, Masters and friends. In doing so they may access their life plan, clear any further blockages and experience a state of absolute bliss and oneness.

Final plunging

Ask the client to create another disk of light above their head:

"Create another disk of light above your head. Compress the light above your head into a disk that is as wide as your body. When it is full and bright take a deep in breath in and on the out breath plunge it slowly down through the body taking time to thank every part of your physical body for enabling you to have this is experience here on Earth now."

Your voice should be soft and reassuring, but still use your normal voice. It should be natural, sincere and clear. Throughout the session you will always use open ended questions. For example "How does that feel?" *Never ask a leading question*, "Do you see your spirit guides?" Always use simple, short, open-ended questions.

Placing crystals on the body

As the client plunges now is the time to place crystals on the body. Warn them you are about to do this if you choose to do so, (if you don't they might be startled when you place crystals on their body). In the simplest sense, a crystal's colour vibration relates to the colour of the chakra. So a typical layout might include (one stone on each chakra) :

Root	Red	Red jasper, iron tiger
Navel	Orange	Carnelian, red jasper
Solar plexus.	Yellow	Citrine, amber, yellow calcite
Heart	Pink/blue/green	Rose quartz/ aquamarine/ malacite
Throat	Green/blue	Turquoise, sodalite, lapis lazuli
Third Eye	Violet	Lepidolite, amethyst, fluorite
Crown	White	Clear quartz, selenite, clear calcite

Each stone is placed on the chakra and connected if possible by a double terminator between each chakra. If not, a single terminator pointing up will suffice. You may use Isis crystals between chakras if you wish. Place a natural, unpolished double terminator between the heart and throat chakras, we want your client to voice their feelings and speak from the heart. Always place grounding stones at the Earth Star.

Once all stones are on and connected with single or double terminators, then you may amplify each stone as you choose with smaller clear quartz points all pointing inwards towards the stone on the centre of the chakra. When all stones are in place and the client is relaxed you are now ready to begin final cleansing. Ensure that stones are not causing any discomfort for the client, if they are, remove and change them.

You may feel to focus on the heart throat and third eye chakras. Providing the heart and throat are connected by a natural double terminator and the lower chakras are clear you can facilitate a profound journey by laying stones on just these three chakras. You may collect a variety of exotic stones for this purpose, experiment and listen to your own higher guidance. Some clients will not require Chakra stones at all.

Third eye and heart chakra stones

Consider placing the following stones on the third eye chakra to assist your clients journey:

- Moldavite, purple fluorite, small elestial, Herkimer diamond, lapis lazuli, clear calcite, clear quartz with chlorite, phantoms or other inclusions, aqua aura, opal aura, aquamarine, natural apophyllite pyramid, labradorite or sugilite.

It is important for spiritual energy to flow freely through the heart, consider placing the following stones over the heart chakra:

- Malachite, aquamarine, clear quartz, rose quartz or lapis.

All of the above stones may prove to be more powerful when shaped as a pyramid, rather than a tumblestone.

Emotional release

At this time if you have placed stones on the heart chakra they may stimulate a spontaneous release of any emotional blockages that are being held by your client, particularly if you have placed malachite there. These blockages may not have shown up in your scanning process. This will manifest by the client at first feeling sad, then weepy. They may not know why.

Just explain that will become apparent if they allow the feelings to come to the surface and release them. Your client may become very emotional at this point as they remember some past deep pain that they have protected

65

themselves from, by saving it until they were ready to deal with it. Depending on what arises you can use the techniques outlined in this book to clear the trauma.

The waterfall

After clearing any other blockages held in the body and when after a re-scan everything is clear, you can suggest:

> *"Take yourself to a beautiful place in nature, where there is a crystal clear waterfall and rock pool. Go and stand under the waterfall and allow it to wash over you, cleansing every part of your body. Move your body round and make sure every part of your body is cleansed. Take a moment to honour the beautiful being of light that you are.*
>
> *How does that feel?*
>
> *When you feel cleansed and refreshed step out of the waterfall and have a look around, tell me about the place you are in. Describe it to me...*
>
> *I am interested to know if you notice anything particularly interesting or beautiful..."*

At this point your client has been purified, and has had a physical, emotional and etheric body healing. They are now in a fit state to consciously meet with more highly evolved beings of light on the spiritual plane in a totally protected environment.

Regardless of what your client may be thinking they are entering an altered state of awareness. Even if your client feels that they are "imagining" their experience, continue with the process regardless as it will create a portal for their consciousness to expand.

We are looking for anything interesting or beautiful as this is the way their team will initiate communication with them, through beauty and love.

Relinquishing control

At this point you relinquish control by suggestion. You encourage the client to explore the environment and let their heart lead them. Always projecting love in front of them as they explore.

The importance of not pre-programming your client now becomes apparent. You should not have indicated anything about what may happen, only that each journey is different and an unpredictable enjoyable adventure. It is important that the client not be creating the situation that they expect through your prior suggestion, but truly exploring a real environment through another part of their consciousness.

Situations which present themselves are as varied as the people who see you, although there is a common pattern. You must now trust that whatever appears in the journey is appropriate for your client. Until your client meets their team you will avoid suggestion, whenever possible.

Reality NOT Symbolism

Your client is on a real plane in real time. Whatever happens is *real, not symbolic.* The beings your client meets are separate sentient beings not constructs of their imagination. I strongly discourage you or your client exploring the symbolism of a journey. We are accessing the superconscious not the subconscious. *Do not analyse* journeys, particularly during a session, you will find you are barking up the wrong tree.

Beyond the waterfall, your questions

Your client will remain in constant communication with you at all times by talking to you and telling you what happens. You will prompt them by *always* asking *open ended questions* eg. "What's happening now?" Not, "Do you see an eagle?" Ask every few minutes.

NEVER LEAD YOUR CLIENT BY SUGGESTION.

It is important that the client feel relaxed and at ease. They do not know it, and you will not tell them, but they are looking for a place where their guides can meet them. In that place they will feel relaxed, comfortable and at ease. That place can be surprisingly varied, from a mountain top, to a cave, to a castle or even a cafe in Paris, France. One client's guides chose to meet her in the boardroom of a high rise corporate headquarters. Your client will probably have an adventure getting there and that is all part of the journey. Encourage them to explore the terrain they find themselves in, they can be bold and adventurous. They should have a good look around for anything which attracts their attention or looks particularly beautiful or interesting and follow where their heart leads.

Guides and their helpers

Early in the journey as your client explores the environment, listen out for contact with any creatures. Animals are frequently messengers or helpers and sometimes guides or totem animals. Your client will be attracted to their simple beauty and playfulness. They will be able to take your client to a sacred place (i.e. a deeper state). It should be obvious that they are loving creatures. If in doubt suggest your client ask:

"Do you love me?"

When you receive a clear and positive response you may ask three times.

"Do you love me unconditionally?"

After receiving a positive unevasive answer each time the question is answered, you can suggest your client give permission for them to assist their journey or they may ask:

"Please take me to a sacred place. I am ready to remember all that I am."

These helpers can take them to a place where they can meet their guides and/or ancestors. Occasionally for a lucky few, the fairies and nature divas help out, a very pleasant experience for all concerned. Sometimes guides appear immediately, often surrounded by bright golden light, or initially perceived as a source of light, behind trees or in a cave or pool. Encourage your client to explore any source of light.

If they are having difficulty perceiving their team clearly they can also say:

"Please take me into a deeper state so I may hear and see you more clearly."

If you do not receive a positive response then the questions your client should ask are:

"What do you want?"

"What is our relationship?"

"When did I give you permission to be here?"

"What is the nature of our agreement?"

The answers to these questions will give you the information you need to facilitate a release which is covered shortly.

It is important to understand that with any first time Crystal Dreaming journey, your client's guides and friends will present in a way that your client feels most comfortable with. So a person with a strong, Hindu, Christian, Jewish or any other faith may initially perceive their guides and teachers in that context. However if they return for subsequent sessions the beings they are interacting with will, in due course, reveal the much bigger interlacing reality that they exist in.

You may discover for example that Celtic Gods and Goddesses have counterparts or other aspects of themselves in all the other ancient and modern faiths or religions. You will never suggest this to any client, you will allow them to discover it for themselves.

At this stage you may also encounter beings who do not love your client unconditionally.

Travelling and asking for help

The client may be told when appropriate that they are not bounded by the laws of this plane. They can fly, or swim underwater without breathing, although generally people discover this for themselves.

Encourage them to be inquisitive and alert and have fun. Above all they should listen to their heart, not their head. They may not immediately meet a helper, this could be because their conscious mind is blocking the journey or they are fearful. They may actually need to go through some kind of initiation or their journey may be being blocked by a negative entity.

At some point, if you have not been assisted in the journey by a creature or messenger they may announce:

"I am ready to meet any being who wishes to meet me here."

Open ended and helpful if you suspect interference or attachment, or:

"I am ready to meet any being that loves me unconditionally."

If an angry or threatening being shows itself, you will need to use the clearing techniques described later in this book. As you have cleared the space prior to the client arriving anything they interact with is with them, not in your space. It is unlikely in the early stages of your work that you will be dealing with many serious or challenging negative attachments or entities. This is because your spiritual team will guide clients to you that you are ready for and able to help.

If you do find yourself constantly challenged by misguided beings, as I was, then you can rest assured that you *are* ready to deal with it, and it is part of your path to do so.

Meeting guides and others

There is usually little doubt when someone meets a guide because the client is surprised by a very warm feeling of love, and sometimes may get a little teary at the reunion. Occasionally some people are tested by their spiritual teachers. If you have any doubt at all as to the motives of any being your client encounters, ask them to ask and wait for a reply three times:

"What is our relationship?"

"Do you love me?"

"Do you love me unconditionally?"

"Are you focused on my divine highest good?"

Once your client has connected with their guides the fun really begins.

You will be able to facilitate as a team member some extraordinary physical, emotional and spiritual healings from this point on.

If your client receives an evasive response to the questions suggested it is an indication that the being you are encountering is not positive. Remember not to allow your client to accept gifts or enter into any agreements with any being unless they be:

.".. *based on unconditional love, for my Divine highest good, the Divine highest good of all and in accordance with the Divine plan. "*

How Guides appear

Guides are lovely people, and like us come in all shapes and sizes. Occasionally just appearing as lights or energy, sometimes as animals, they most frequently appear as human. Usually dressed as they were in their prime, during the incarnation when they were closest to your client.

All Spirit Guides are friends, relatives, ancestors or spouses we have actually incarnated with in the past. Every one of them loves us unconditionally and each has a special relationship with us. It is not unusual for people to have Native American guides as not only were these a beautiful race who were one with Spirit, many of us have incarnated as Native Americans in the past. Naturally our friends are here to help us.

Guides will be from a variety of cultures and of both sexes, sometimes children as well as elders can appear as guides. If your client notices a priest or priestess, shaman, magician or medicine woman in their team then chances are they have these abilities themselves. Remember your client will have incarnated *at least once* with each guide.

It can be fun and also very moving to ask individual guides to show your client when they spent time in bodies together:

"Show me when we spent time together and what we did together. I have completely forgotten."

They will take your client back and show them how they lived. If you choose to do this, suggest your client observe closely the detail of the scene unfolding before them.

If your client meets a group of people and all the guides want to speak at once, ask that one step forward as a spokesperson for the whole group, one who may be particularly close to your client. They can in due course speak with them all one at a time.

How guides can help

Guides are able to check all the work done so far and ensure your client is clear of all negative influences and attachments. This is the first thing you should do with them, when you meet them, without fail.

They are also able to show your client their life plan or blueprint. They can assist with travel to other realms. They can assist with challenges on this plane, they can certainly explain to your client why they are choosing to experience these challenges. They can travel through time and space, they can diagnose illness or potential illness, facilitate healings and advise your client about self healings, recommend cures and send healing energy. They can introduce your client's Higher Self and Spiritual teachers. They can, if appropriate, introduce your client to an Ascended Master or other highly evolved loving Spirit beings (Angels). They can assist in bringing in inter-dimensional technologies back to this plane for humanities evolution. They can remove stubborn energy blockages and assist with the release of past life trauma.

As facilitator you can help by suggesting questions to the client who may become overwhelmed on first meeting. After having your clients team check all the work you have done in the session so far, you should always give clear and unambiguous requests and also for the client to give their permission for their guides to interact with them:

> *"Providing you love me unconditionally, I give my permission for my guides to guide and protect me, be close to me and send me healing energies."*

Guides and teachers can help with life on this plane in many ways. I suggest the focus to be on reconnecting with the client's life purpose or blueprint and how that in turn will best serve our evolution as a species. A good question for your client is:

> *"I am ready to activate my life plan in service to light and unconditional love. Please show me what changes I should make in my life to allow this to flow with ease and grace."*

You may suggest, if it be appropriate and if it has not happened spontaneously, that your client be escorted to the Source of all Light and love and shown how the Universe works. Quite an experience! There are more suggestions in Chapter Ten.

Spontaneous past life recall

Some clients may move into a past life recall spontaneously upon leaving the waterfall. Your attempts to connect them to their guides through messengers or totem animals will not work as they will not appear as such. In past life recall, your client will experience a vivid reliving of a particular and relevant experience. They will be smelling, feeling and seeing everything in a heightened sense, everything will be crystal clear.

They will often see themselves in a situation taking part in some activity. Even though they may be a different age or sex, they will usually realise that they are witnessing themselves in a past life.

"How does your body feel? Is it male or female?"

"Look down at your body, what are you wearing?"

"Tell me what is going on around you, how are people dressed? What are they doing? What tools are they using?"

"Do you recognise anyone's energy?"

If their body experiences pain or a traumatic death and it becomes unbearable for your client you can simply suggest that they step out of the body they are in and observe the event from the outside.

Whilst in a past life recall your client's perception of the detail of the scene unfolding will usually be staggering in its clarity. In looking at the key players in a scene they may be surprised to notice that a close friend or relative is with them in another guise. Do not lead this discovery, by suggesting that this might be the case, let them discover it for themselves.

Past life recall can serve as a useful illustration of why a particular situation is repeatedly manifesting in your client's life. In any recall your focus is on changing the way your client *feels* about a particular experience. You cannot change the experience itself.

In terms of helping your client clear any trauma ask yourself: How can I apply forgiveness in this situation?

Finishing the Session

Before finishing, suggest the client ask for a tool or method of contacting their guides after your session. It is always given. Watch the time and your client's well-being. Bi-locating, for the uninitiated can be very tiring. Advise your client to let their guides know if the body is feeling tired or distressed, particularly if they are taken on an interstellar journey.

Allow up to one and a half hours for a session. After about one and a quarter hours, tell your client that you will be finishing soon and if they want to ask any final questions or say goodbyes, now is the time. They should stand and give thanks from the heart for all the energies and beings they have encountered:

"Notice a rainbow nearby and fly into it or ask your team to lift you up and place you in it. Float in it's colours, allowing the colours

to balance, harmonise and energise your body. Allow yourself to slide down the rainbow and slip back into your physical body through the top of your head.

Feeling fingers, toes, bones, muscles, breath, crystals on your body, gently stretching, slowly open your eyes and become fully present here with me."

Centre yourself and give thanks to the spiritual teams saying out loud:

"I give thanks to _____'s spiritual guides, teachers and friends. I give thanks to my own spiritual guides, teachers and friends, my own mastery and my own Higher Self. Thank you all for being with us today. Thank you for sharing with us, your healing energies and protection. I give thanks, in full faith. So be it."

Post Session Discussion

For most clients their Crystal Dreaming session will have a profound and immediate effect on them. If you have guided it appropriately then they should not need to ask many questions. However some clients will want to ask questions. I suggest you ask all clients to honour the journey by not questioning the truth of what they experienced during their journey. It was not a symbolic journey through the subconscious so there is no need to analyse it.

Often it helps if they can write their experience down. It may also help you to keep notes. I recommend you familiarise yourself with some of the energies and beings they are likely to encounter through further reading.

Have a cleansed ball of iron tiger, red jasper or hematite for your client to hold after the session. Holding a grounding and nurturing stone will assist with their integration of the session. They should not drive immediately after a session, suggest they rest, eat, walk or have a break before driving a car. They may also feel quite tired later in the day. Encourage them to take it easy and relax for the rest of the day if possible.

Finishing off at the end of the day

Cleanse all crystals that have touched the body after each session in fresh water and with prana or Reiki. Express your thanks from the heart as you repeat the cleansing exercise in Chapter Six.

Payment for healings

It is important that your "practice" clients value their experience. It is very appropriate to swap, barter or trade services or gifts, for example; a massage, dinner, a car clean etc. Do not give healings away unless to a very special person. It is important that people want a healing, value it and are prepared to exchange something for it.

Conclusion

Crystal Dreaming can lead to a blissful reunion with spirit and provided you work with the purest intentions always, you will achieve positive if not miraculous healing results. In the next chapter we will look at some of the things you can do with your client once you have connected them with their team.

Chapter 10
Challenges and solutions

The aim of all Crystal Dreaming sessions is to reunite your clients with a beautiful and powerful state of oneness and bliss in which profound healing may take place. The journeys your clients experience will be as many and varied as the individuals involved. Crystal Dreaming is capable of transporting any human being into a state of joy that is indescribable.

Human beings, however, being the complex creatures that we are, create many blocks to this reunion with Source. By its nature this technique will present all blockages that prevent access to bliss for removal during the session. In the next two chapters we will examine some possible routes a journey might take and the challenges you may be presented with during the course of your Crystal Dreaming sessions.

Some Universal truths of the Spirit world

- We are all Spirit beings having a human experience.
- Our consciousness is infinite, it is not limited by time or space.
- Earth is a school that we come to in order to learn who we are.
- All beings around and on this planet have individual free will.
- All beings throughout the universe are bound to the truth.
- *Nothing* has power over us unless we allow it.

Those who can not go

Occasionally you will encounter people who have difficulty responding to this technique. These are fortunately few, (approximately one in ten) and they are probably either fearful or are in the mind and need to be guided into the heart. Clients often expect a full technicolour movie show when in fact if they listen to what their feelings are telling them they will have a profound experience. There is usually enough information in feelings to translate into a story that from your position sounds totally visual. The "pictures" will come through their feelings if they allow their hearts to open and describe how they feel.

Remember do not use the word "see" use "perceive", it is more open ended. Some useful questions are:

> *"How do you feel?"*
> *"What is the heavy thing on your chest made of?"*
> *"What kind of environment are you in?"*

"Feel your body, is it male or female?"

"What are wearing?"

"What is causing the sharp pain in your back, feel into it, what is it made of?"

"What is the solid ball in your throat made of? What colour is it?"

Remember also that fear of the unknown or an entity may be blocking the journey, in which case, if all else fails, your client may say:

"I challenge any being that is under the illusion that it has power over me. Show yourself to me NOW!"

That usually provokes a response!

Chakra cleansing

One way of gently helping your client into the appropriate space is the following chakra cleansing meditation. It is enough that your client intend the following if they insist that they can't see it, apart from being very relaxing and refreshing it may open them up to the full Crystal Dreaming experience.

Repeat the plunging process or follow straight on from it.

"Breathe in light through the flower above your head and draw it down through the centre of the body to the root chakra in the front of the body, there open a beautiful soft red flower, allow the light you are breathing out to blow out any dust or cobwebs as the flower opens."

Work your way up through the chakras, navel - orange flower, solar plexus - yellow flower, heart - pink, blue or green flower, throat - turquoise flower, third eye - violet flower, crown, - white flower. Your client will then command all the chakras to stabilise and continue with the second part of this process.

"Drawing light through the crown, take it down to your power centre or Hara, a hands breadth below the navel in the centre of your body. There build a star pushing out light with every out breath. Allow it to grow filling your body, pushing out shafts of light in every direction, dissolving any energies not totally aligned with light.

When your body is full of light, extend light beyond your body, creating an egg-shape all around you. Allow that to fill with light.

When the egg is complete, see yourself bathing in a cool violet flame, then see a violet flame licking the outside of your egg, leaving a violet hue.

When that feels comfortable create a sparkling gold see-through criss-cross mesh on the outside of the egg and then create a platinum mesh on top of that. You may declare that this mesh will only let love and light in and will repel all other thought forms.

Now project a ray of pink from your own heart projecting unconditional love for all things. Allow that to spread out from your heart, forming a bubble that surrounds your whole being. You may declare out loud,

"I am light,
I am love,
I am protected."

By this time your client may well be perceiving a great deal and you may attempt to continue the Crystal Dreaming process. If not they are probably very much in their body, in the room with you, in which case you may suggest they stretch and open their eyes. You may then debrief and consider suggesting another modality.

You may take your client through the second part of this process at any time during a session. It is a great exercise to give your client to remember if they are prone to fear. It is an exercise I recommend be carried out morning and evening every day, for anyone.

Do not be concerned if your client does not respond to the Crystal Dreaming process, not all healing modalities work for everyone, it is no reflection on your technique, providing it does not happen frequently. You may ask for a donation for your time or not charge anything for the part session they have experienced. It is not appropriate to charge for a full session.

Usually you will know within half an hour whether you should stop a session because it is not working for your client.

Those who won't come back

Occasionally you will encounter someone whose experience of total bliss is so profound, they will refuse to return. This can turn into a real challenge if you do not tackle it immediately and forcefully.

Firmly and calmly remind them of their promise made at the start of the session. Remind them of those who love them on this plane, especially children, reminding them that it is not yet their time to leave this plane etc. KEEP THEM TALKING.

As you do so, start dismantling the grid around the client, starting at the crown, remove all stones around the body or turn the points away from the body. *Leave the hematite,* and any other grounding stones where they are. Leave the crystal balls at the top and bottom of the body but dismantle the lines of stones above and below the body.

Then remove any stones on the body and get every grounding stone you have and place them on the lower and upper chakras, particularly the hip joints, below the knees, ankles and feet. Tell them what you are doing.

"I am placing grounding stones on your body which will bring you back into full consciousness. You are returning to your body now, the crystals around your body have all been removed, it is time to come back."

This is the only time you will use suggestion and extend your will over your client. Gently remove the crystals from the hands and replace with hematite or similar grounding stones.

Do not move them or shake them as they have left their body and the shock may be detrimental to their health. Be firm and clear as you talk to them, they WILL come back into their body, now. Do not lose contact with them and do not lose your cool either, *keep them talking.*

If you need to, ask your whole team to help get them back in their body. You may also ask their own guides to assist with this process, and any other loving being that you or they may be attuned to.

If you suspect that this situation is about to occur, act sooner rather than later. As all clients lose track of time you can start by saying that it is time to return as the session is almost over. When they return, they will be very emotional and probably very angry with you for spoiling their fun. You may have to suspend giving them a piece of your mind till later.

This situation is rare but it can happen, so be aware.

Too much information, too fast

For some clients this process is like releasing a dam of multiple, overlaid experiences and they are overwhelmed by multiple recalls of different situations and emotions, They find themselves flipping from life to life, particularly with repeated, unresolved traumas, over several incarnations. The key here is to focus on the primary trauma. Your client may say:

"Body I command you, take me to the moment this series of traumas started."

OR *"Body, Take me to the moment this first happened to me."*

Entities appearing after contact with guides

This is unusual, but it can happen. It may be that the entity has been holding back not wanting to be discovered, not realising how well trained you are. Occasionally it can be a test constructed by your client's own spiritual teachers. Find out as much as you can about the entity and why it is with your client who may dissolve any agreements made with the entity and suggest it return home to light.

You may also ask the client's team why the entity is there. Use your discretion and use the advanced techniques described later if you need to. Remember the only way an entity can appear is if they are already attached to the client. Provided you follow the method of preparation I have outlined it is impossible for beings not aligned with light and love to penetrate your sacred space from the outside.

Accessing past life recall

The easiest way to access a past life experience is via your client's spiritual team. Once you have established a clear rapport with your client's team and checked all the work you have done so far, you simply ask them, providing it be appropriate and for their Divine highest good, that your client's guides take them to or show them a past life experience or skills which are relevant to this life.

This is a good exercise for clients who you sense are having difficulty believing the truth of the altered state they are experiencing. A past life recall with its clarity will leave them in no doubt whatsoever about the truth of reincarnation or the information they are receiving through the altered state you have facilitated. Ask them to study the detail of what they are seeing and tell you about it.

Past life recall is useful in helping your client understand the skills and challenges they may have brought into this life.

Transmigration of spirits

Very occasionally you may come across an individual who experiences a life as an animal in a past life recall. A person may transmigrate to the animal kingdom for one or more incarnations to work out or release a large amount of negative Karma accrued during the previous life as a human being. So if a person was particularly cruel or base in a human life they may be offered the choice of incarnating as an animal to experience the suffering that they perpetrated first hand.

I have dealt with clients who are made aware of relationships with others who have interacted with them in past lives as animals, and are presently incarnated once more as humans and with people who experienced an incarnation as an animal.

Meeting positive ETs and interdimensionals

As a general rule it is best to allow clients to find their own way of interacting with positive loving extraterrestrials or interdimensionals as your session unfolds. However you may encounter clients who have a specific request to meet interdimensionals or extraterrestrials in which case you should do this via their team. In fact you would expect a member of their team to be an ET. In any interaction with ETs you should *always* ask the appropriate questions three times of any being your client meets.

> *"Do you love me? Do you love me unconditionally?"*

Positive beings are loving and patient and will understand your insistence on receiving three separate confirmations that they love your client unconditionally and are focused on their Divine highest good.

You cannot control or force an interaction with ETs. If your client is not ready for it, it will not happen. Before you attempt such a meeting, your client should already have met with their own team.

Blocks to a journey

Not all blocks are caused by earthbound spirits or negative entities and unless you suspect spirit attachment it is a good idea to investigate other possibilities first. Your client may have made an agreement with themselves not to experience fully their own psychic abilities because of persecution or torture in a past life.

Your client or their ancestors may have drawn up a contract with a circle, society or group that they will not align themselves with light, unconditional love or their Divine plan.

Your client will be either totally unaware of these blocks or may have a vague feeling of unease around recollection of what they might be. This is because they have locked the memory into the cells of their body until they are ready to release it:

> *"I now dissolve all agreements I may have made with myself for my own protection."*

Or

> *"I now dissolve all agreements that may have been made on my behalf before I was born."*

Or

> *"I now dissolve all agreements I may have made or that have been made on my behalf with any circle or society in a past life relating to my lineage. I revoke all past life contracts that are not part of my Divine plan or totally aligned with light."*

Your client may need to have a dialogue with their ancestors or other members of the group, in order to clarify that they are now aware that they are a sovereign being of light with free will, who has decided to take control of their life.

Releasing a block

In the early stages of a blocked journey eg. your client steps out of the waterfall and sees absolutely nothing or they spend half an hour wandering around obviously in an altered state but not encountering any other beings, animals, fish or birds, your client could try the following affirmation:

"I challenge any being that is under the illusion that it has power over me show yourself to me NOW!

OR relinquish your power and forever hold your peace."

It usually triggers a response.

Karma

In uncovering a past life trauma you may discover a Karmic issue that can be resolved. Often it is enough to call on the spirit of the wronged person and ask for both forgiveness and for the Karma to be lifted. Providing your client is genuine in begging forgiveness and the wronged spirit agrees of their own free will that your client has suffered enough, the Karma may be considered balanced and released. If this is then verified by a higher authority (eg. your clients spiritual teacher or team) then your client is free from the challenges that the past life karma was creating in their lives now, from that moment on, instantly.

See the case study "Stubborn and mysterious illness."

Karmic court

Not all karma issues are so simple. Sometimes you need to ask for a hearing at a Karmic court. As there is no time-space in the spirit world, as soon as you ask for a hearing in the Karmic court you will receive one.

The court will appear to your client like a magistrates courtroom with several Ascended beings sitting behind a bench on a raised dais:

"Approach the court with respect. Advise them we are here to plead your case. We are requesting the Karma we have just become aware of now be considered to be cleared.

Advise them you have been totally forgiven by those involved and all ties to the trauma have been voluntarily released by all parties concerned.

Say that we now respectfully plead clemency, and ask to be released from this Karma."

The court may go into discussion and ask questions. You will act as a barrister, helping your client plead their case for the permanent release of their Karma. The client may repeat what you say out loud or if things are moving quickly, they may just transmit what you say to the court. They can hear your comments and suggestions through the client anyway.

Your client may need to offer a period of community service, or at least be open to the court's demands. Feeding the poor or needy is a rapid way to clear Karma.

See the case study "Karma."

Ancient Gods and Goddesses

Your client may find themselves in an ancient temple meeting powerful ancient or mythical Gods or Goddesses. These Gods may wish to speak through your client or remind your client of an ancient agreement to serve them. *Proceed with caution.*

The ancient ones did not always love us unconditionally. They may have loved us as their children (which we may well be) but you will find that they often have an agenda. Find out as much as you can about your client's relationship with them and what they want from your client and humanity. Your client will no doubt become emotional at their reunion, it is likely that your client was totally devoted to them. Do not let this influence their choices now.

The ancient Egyptians were a particularly powerful group, so be aware. Fortunately they understand that agreements can be dissolved and they do generally respect our free will. Should an ancient one take over your client's body and speak through them during a session without their conscious permission, you will need to remind them of your client's sovereignty, the time and place now and request they leave, calling on your client to re-occupy their body as you do so.

If your client does wish to channel the being then agree on a specific time limit (ten minutes) and request that the being use the client's vocabulary and speak in English, otherwise you may not be able to understand them.

Soul family trauma

We are so close to members of our own soul family that their trauma can affect us and sometimes we can release it for them. If your client is having a graphic first hand experience which appears illogical then release the trauma as you would any other trauma, even though the time line may not make sense to you in the moment. Refer to the "Disco inferno" case study in the appendix for an example of how this can manifest.

Soul braiding

You will occasionally in your practice encounter people who have a profound realisation, often through a graphic past life recall, that they have been, or are, a highly evolved or Ascended being. This needs some explanation.

In these times of great change it is a far more efficient use of energy and power to split the consciousness of an Ascended Master and braid it with the spirits of those souls who are evolved enough to incarnate and deal with it. You can ask that your client be shown how this works if either of you doubt it. An Ascended Master can be and reincarnate in many bodies simultaneously. They can also travel incognito until their special skills are needed. At which point your client will be reminded of who they are and why they came here.

Soul braiding is planned before birth and is triggered by the clearance of all Karma in your client. A blessed state! This realisation can happen during Crystal Dreaming sessions. This being the case the biggest thing your client is likely to have to deal with is worthiness issues.

Often the recall that triggers this realisation is connected to a past life trauma or death that is locked into your clients cellular memory until the appropriate time to release it. The best way to guide a client through this experience is to first release the memory as advised earlier. As they re-experience the event in question suggest they affirm:

"Everything is perfect, I honour my choice to have (or witness) this experience. I understand that I know nothing of the Divine plan and where this may lead and I accept that everything is perfect. All my choices were perfect. I thank my cells for retaining this memory, it has served its purpose, I now accept all that I am.

I now affirm that I no longer need to hold on to this memory as it no longer serves me. I release this cellular memory now, to be transmuted into light for the divine highest good of all. So be it!"

Having released this cellular memory it is now appropriate for your client to accept who they are and/or why they were witnessing, or involved with, the situation they have just recalled. This can be both humbling and confusing for your client. Accepting that you are a powerful being can be challenging!

It is true, they are *part* of the consciousness they recall being and as such it is likely they will have specific work to achieve once their Karma is completely clear. Ask their own team to explain it to them.

Your client will receive information about their special role in our planet's evolution during the rest of their Crystal Dreaming session.

Multiple incarnation trauma release

If one of your client's multiple incarnations is killed traumatically it is possible to release this trauma in a Crystal Dreaming session, as you all come directly from the same consciousness and are interconnected. Should this arise in any session treat the trauma release as you would any other.

What won't make sense at the time is the time line and how the client appears (eg. obviously present day but the client appears to be a peasant labourer in China). Later in the session have the clients team explain how it all works. The key for you as the therapist is to clear the trauma as it presents during a session, even if it does not make complete sense at that moment.

Non-human trauma release

Any client can move into a trauma release in another time-space continuum in which they do not appear to be human. Work on the release as you would any other trauma and later in the session have their team explain what was happening to them.

Pregnant women and unborn babies

Do not offer a Crystal Dreaming session to pregnant women. There is no need for the unborn child to go through the mother's trauma release. If the pregnant woman is a close friend and keen to experience Crystal Dreaming you may refer them to an Advanced practitioner.

During her Advanced session she will be advised that the incoming spirit of the child that they contact is *probably* the spirit which will occupy the child's body. If the family's circumstances change dramatically during pregnancy then the requirements of the family and the incoming spirit will also change. The final bonding between body and spirit does not take place until the child is close to birth. Having said this in most cases the spirit the mother interacts with will be the same as the one that is born as her child.

This understanding can be enlightening and moving for all concerned as the child will explain why s/he chose the family and what they hope to achieve with them.

Working with children

It is not appropriate to offer a Crystal Dreaming session to anyone under the age of eighteen. In the case of clients who have challenges with children you may with the child's permission work on them through either of the parents; or, with both the child's and the parent's permission, someone close to the child who loves them very much.

You will advise the client that they will have to go through the whole process themselves before you can work on the child. Once they are clear and connected with their team you then call on the child's team and instructing your client work on the child through both teams. This process works very well with immediate results.

The child does not need to be present during the session although the child should be supervised wherever they are at the time of the healing.

Absentee healings

Working with a qualified Crystal Dreaming practitioner, use the same techniques and protocols described above, having first obtained the absentee client's permission.

Carry out the normal Crystal Dreaming process with another Crystal Dreaming practitioner taking the role of the "parent" as described above. Once they are clear and have connected with their team, view and heal the absentee client, working with the client's team. When it is not possible to work with a client in person, this technique can achieve profound and immediate results.

Research

Using the same techniques and protocols and working with a qualified practitioner it is also possible to carry out research into a variety of subjects. Travelling through time and space with their team, clients who have experienced several Crystal Dreaming sessions and are clear, may wish to do this.

Working alone

Never practice on yourself.

NEVER LIE IN THE MANDALA ALONE.

It is dangerous to attempt a journey alone without a trained Crystal Dreaming facilitator. On request I will train experienced facilitators how to do this, but they must have been practicing at least one year before being considered. You should always have a qualified Crystal Dreaming facilitator in the room with you, assisting your journey.

Conclusion

You now have an understanding of the more complex issues that you will encounter as your abilities develop. You understand the power of affirmations and how important it is to remain detached and compassionate during your sessions.

It is now time for us to explore the most challenging aspect of Crystal Dreaming: That is the release of the more aggressive negative entities that are always revealed, as the alchemy of crystals shifts your client's consciousness into a higher vibrational reality.

Chapter 11
Helping aggressive entities

I advise you learn they key affirmations provided in this section by heart. When you need to use them you may not have the time to refer to a page in this book, at the very least copy them in large print and have them close at hand. Please do not be daunted by this section, I must include this information because in due course if you practice these techniques you will encounter similar situations, this text would be incomplete without it.

It would be very unusual for you to encounter this work early in your practice, if you do, you are ready to deal with it.

Psychic Attack

Any person may at any point in their life come under psychic attack. Psychic attack is defined as any attempt to intrude on a beings sovereignty and influence them negatively by focusing negative energy or thought forms on them. It can manifest in the subject as repeated nightmares, nausea, inexplicable pains in the neck and other parts of the body, headaches, pains in the solar plexus or stomach and uneasiness or fear. Humans become vulnerable to attack when they become weak or fearful, or have an addiction to drugs or alcohol, or use recreational drugs such as marijuana or LSD.

As a Crystal Dreaming practitioner you will without doubt, at some stage, come under attack as misguided beings attempt to stop your work. Whilst experiencing an attack can be disturbing it is not hard to deal with and is not normally life threatening.

Any being misguided enough to be abusing their power by trying to cause another being pain or suffering is operating in a fear based reality. Those operating in this reality are repulsed by the higher vibration of love. So for your own personal protection, should you feel under attack, visualise etheric mirrors around yourself and your home, mirrors that have a coating of love and a wish for enlightenment for all the negative energies they reflect. In this way you return any negative intentions to the sender, with a supercharged coating of love and wishes for enlightenment.

Those of you who have encountered misguided individuals who are dabbling in black magic may have wondered why they look so tired. It is not only because the negative entities they bargain with take a heavy toll, it is because they very often receive back the negative energies and thought forms they have sent out. Those of us projecting thoughts of love and wishes for enlightenment, have nothing to fear if they are sent back to us.

Take any form of psychic attack as a compliment, you are worthy of attention, you are doing your job well. Your light is shining brightly and revealing those that have become lost in the shadows.

Dream intrusion

As your skills and power develop you may find that occasionally your dreams are invaded by others. These could include ETs, earthbound spirits, reptoids, military personnel and living sorcerers or witches. The latter will have become aware of your activities on their "patch" and will be trying to intimidate you.

The aim of any invasion is to scare you off and the best way to deal with it is *in the dream*. That means as soon as you become aware of any funny business, rather than waking up in a cold sweat, you interact in the dream state. Or if you do wake up, return to the dream state immediately. Remember it is your dream not theirs; you are in control. They are trying to influence your thoughts to create the illusion of fear, once you are aware of this you can have some fun.

Any restraining devices or bonds are an illusion, snap them like cotton. Any feeling of powerlessness is an illusion, make yourself bigger and stronger. Confront the invaders; stretch out your arm and release a bolt or stream of white prana directly at them from the palm of your hand. The rest will come to you in the moment, it is your dream, you are in control.

Possession

Possession is an extreme form of spirit attachment. In this situation the attached spirit is not lost or confused and is well aware of the situation, having no intention of ever transiting to the next level of consciousness. The possessing spirit controls the host's life by impelling them through their emotions to behave in a way that entertains the spirit or gives it pleasure or energy. Often recreating situations that gave it a thrill whilst alive, it may lead people to do the most bizarre and misguided things imaginable.

Most frequently victims find themselves subject to deep irrational fears, murderous thoughts or contemplation of suicide. This situation can and does happen to the nicest of people and when it is detected it can usually be dealt with, permanently, in one session.

Ten indicators of spirit attachment or possession:
1   Deep seated irrational fears
2   Murderous thoughts and suicidal tendencies
3   Obsessive or compulsive behaviour

4   Hearing voices that do not say positive things

5   Lethargy, listlessness, lack of vitality or depression

6   Continued addictions that refuse treatment

7   Violent temper erupting for no apparent reason

8   Continued sexual dysfunction or obsession

9   Psychic abilities that focus on the negative

10   Repeated nightmares in which the same person appears

The types of spirit who attach to your client with the conscious intention to possess them are varied. Here are some examples:

- A murderer, rapist and torturer dies; he is terrified of retribution for his cruel acts if he transits, so he refuses the opportunity. He witnesses how other spirits trick people into making an agreement. This he does, and proceeds to make someone's life a living hell.

- A junkie overdoses in a toilet in Kings Cross, she drifts out of her body not really knowing if she is alive or dead. She sees her guides but dismisses them as a hallucination. Eventually she realises that she is dead. By this time it is too late to make the transition, she drifts around until she finds another stoned junkie she can trick into letting her attach and continue her junkie experience.

- Similarly an alcoholic dies in a stupor. He too will seek and find another alcoholic to attach to, continuing his ongoing love affair with the bottle.

- An intelligent and experienced black magician or witch dies after a misguided life based on ego, greed and power over others. They are well aware of the death and transition process and have planned to stay earthbound fearing retribution and not wanting to end the fun they are having frightening people on Earth. They move from one host to another impelling them to suicide or murder until they get bored and find somebody else.

- A person becomes deeply depressed and takes their own life. They are in such a state when they die that they refuse the opportunity to transit not believing it to be possible, they then look for a similarly depressed person to attach to.

- A man lives life to the full, fast cars, fast women, lots of possessions, parties and sensual pleasures. Death comes unexpectedly when this person is in their prime having lots of three dimensional fun. They refuse point blank to leave when they die and spend years hanging around with similar people, until eventually they find one to attach to.

• A person is killed violently or tragically, left for dead when they are still alive. They die an agonisingly slow and painful death and they are full of anger at the situation they find themselves in. The anger prevents them from transiting and so they become stuck in a permanent state of fear and anger looking for a host.

• A person becomes involved, for kicks, in a magic circle. The leader of the circle is a misguided individual who is enjoying the power over others that this circle gives them. During a ritual the subject is led into making an affirmation or agreement to serve another misguided discarnate being. The agreement is made and is binding.

This list goes on, I am sure you will in due course add to it yourself. The common factor in all cases will be that at some stage your client gave permission for the spirit to attach itself to him/ her consciously or unconsciously, through fear or through love, it does not matter, until the agreement is dissolved by your client the agreement will remain, and so will the spirit.

Indications of possession

As in the indications of spirit attachment mentioned earlier, in cases of possession you will come under attack yourself. This will manifest as stabbing pains, headaches or a feeling of tightness in your solar plexus, as if someone was scrunching it up and twisting it. This is the Earthbound spirit trying to simulate a feeling of fear in your systems. Do not accept it as real fear, clean the chakra and "cut" the area in front of it drawing in light through the crown and projecting it out of the chakra.

Encouraging an entity to come forward

At any point during a session your client can say:

"I welcome help with this journey from any being close to me, please help me NOW."

Or

"If any being wishes to meet me here, show yourself to me now. I would like to thank you and help you."

Often they will step forward and take the opportunity to talk with your client and tell them what to do. They may even act like a spirit guide but their selfish agenda will reveal their true nature.

Another option is to use the affirmation mentioned earlier.

"I challenge any being that is under the illusion that it has power over me show yourself to me NOW!"

This usually gets a response if an entity is present.

Helping confused entities

Always be kind but firm in all dealings with Earthbound spirits. They need to understand and feel from your energy, that you do not intend to harm them and that you can help them. You must also project an air of authority. This will assist your client in understanding that they can overcome the challenge before them.

THINK CAREFULLY BEFORE YOU SPEAK.

At first the attached spirit may not be aware of your skills, so in a roundabout way you should find out when the spirit and your client became "friends" (attachment took place). Ask for your client to be shown a replay or recall of the situation, so they can understand how permission was given.

In cases of possession the attached spirit may be aggressive and fearful. You may need to reassure any Earthbound spirit that you are not going to hurt it. A very empowering affirmation for your client is:

"Don't be afraid. I promise not to hurt you. Tell me what you want, I can help you."

You may ask the spirit what year it is, as they will think it is the year they left their body or you may even ask the following question:

"What year is it? What is the last thing you remember? Do you realise you are dead?"

Even with an aggressive being your client may be reluctant to let it go, as they have become co-dependent. You must also explain to your client that this attachment is stifling their own growth and that of the spirit and preventing connection to their own spirit guides. The client should genuinely thank the spirit for its help regardless of how aggressive it may be and wish it well on its journey home into light.

You will explain to the spirit that it is time to leave and that you are sending it to a much nicer place than your client. If you can find out the spirits name you or your client may name them as you call on their guides for help. Your client should state clearly:

"I call on _____ 's spirit guides.
I call on _____ 's spirit guides.

I call on _____'s spirit guides."

If you don't have a name you may say "this person/being's guides."

Your client will see either lights or people approach, you must reassure the spirit and encourage them to leave with their friends. Tell them not to fear those who have come to help.

BE REASSURING AND COMPASSIONATE TOWARDS AGGRESSIVE ENTITIES, THEY ARE AFRAID.

Your work may not be over at this point as once a person's auric field has been weakened by one attachment it creates space for others, so be aware that any spirits appearing fit the criteria and tests you already know for guides. By the end of the session your client should be reunited with their spirit guides who will check your work and complete the healing. Finish the session by helping your client cleanse and seal their own aura. (Use the self protection that you use before every session, as outlined earlier).

After the session you must counsel your client that they may be feeling a bit empty or sad for the next few days or week. It is vital that whenever they notice this feeling to fill the space with feelings of unconditional love, the kind of feelings generated when they think of those dearest to them. The emptiness will fade over the next week or so and it is worth it because now they will be able to live life to the full and reach their full potential. They should feel free to call you if they need to.

Stubborn entities

Occasionally you will encounter a stubborn spirit, which may do its best to make your client as uncomfortable as possible. It must get a very clear feeling from your client that s/he is aware of their presence and its time for it to leave, this you must do with love. Stubborn spirits may not be angry, they may just have been with your client for a long time and find it hard to leave, indeed it is not unusual for your client to have similar feelings and become very emotional as they part. It is important that your client is ready to let them go

It is very likely that a stubborn entity is afraid of retribution or punishment. Be compassionate and help them understand that there is no retribution in the peaceful place where you are helping them to go to:

*"Don't be afraid, no one here wants to hurt you or trick you.
There is no retribution where you are going, only peace and love."*

Never force a client to release an Earthbound spirit, advise them. It is entirely their choice and not your place to interfere. What do you know about their Karma? In one case I discovered much to my surprise that the very conservative and upright client was as good as possessed. After counselling during the session she refused to part from her attached spirit and the situation remains unresolved.

Any stubborn or angry entity is frightened. Be patient, counsel them and help them understand that you are not going to hurt them in any way. The spirit may not stay with your client without their permission. Both you and your client need to believe this wholeheartedly. It may be necessary at this point to make the following affirmation, which is very powerful.

Affirmation for breaking all agreements

This key affirmation you should learn by heart, you may be called upon to use it when your hands are full! It may trigger a physical reaction in your client. If they are laying down, their body may twist and contort, they may feel nausea or stabbing pains, headaches, a full bladder, extremely hot or cold, they may feel any sensation that the entity can simulate in order to stop the healing. They will need reassurance that this is an illusion that will pass, which it will, as you persuade the entity that you are not going to hurt it.

Your client must repeat the following affirmation out loud with all their heart:

"I_____ of my own free will now dissolve any and all agreements I may have made consciously or unconsciously, with any negative energy or entity, earthbound spirit, alien or reptoid on any plane at any time. Thank you for your service, thank you for teaching me my limitations, thank you for helping me grow, I no longer need you. Please leave me now, please go to the light with love, or show yourself to me and tell me what you want, NOW!"

You may find a person makes almost all of this affirmation fairly casually and then as they reach the last few words they break down in fear or deep sadness. As you have them in an altered state they will immediately see the attached spirit.

Do not take any nonsense from an angry or frightened spirit, tell your client that this situation is about to end and not to be frightened. If the spirit is trying to frighten you and your client remember that *anger is a manifestation of fear.* A great affirmation for your client at this point is:

"Don't be afraid I promise not to harm you."

It can stop the entity in its tracks and also reminds your client that they are the ones with the power in this situation. Be firm and clear but as gentle as you can; you would like to talk with the spirit, you can help them. You are not going to hurt them you would like to hear their story.

Expect to hear all sorts of descriptions that are designed to frighten you and your client. Do not take any notice of them, persevere and explain that you can help and that is why you are talking to them. You are not angry with them and you are not going to hurt them.

Remember *knowledge is power,* the more you know about the entity the more you are in a position to make suggestions that will calm it down. Be patient and persistent.

If these reactions become extreme; a torrent of verbal abuse in a completely different voice or language, actual vomiting or physicalisation of the attached spirit, or extreme facial or body contortions, that appear impossible, you have a challenge that you are ready to deal with.

It would not be happening in your space if your team did not think you were ready.

Remind the client that they are in control and that you only wish to speak with the presence not wrestle with it. Ask them who they are and what they are doing with your client and what they want from them.

You may even need to internally recite the fear affirmation stay calm, you can deal with it:

> *"I choose to live in a fear free environment. I acknowledge my fear as a powerful friend that makes me alert and ready for action, and I thank it for serving me. However, fear does not control me.*
>
> *I choose to centre myself in love and light, I choose to live love, be and share love. Nothing has power over me on this or any other plane. I am a sovereign being of light, my power is limitless. I choose peace, I choose joy, I choose love. Now."*

Be compassionate, the most angry and fearful spirit wants someone to listen to their story; they are stuck. You can help them. Even the meanest sorcerer gets bored messing peoples lives up. You can offer them the challenge of a different experience that they are strong enough to deal with, stepping into the light.

Whatever your approach, the key to your success is your compassion, love, patience, understanding and lack of fear.

You will, after using lots of initiative, locate and help many confused spirits, often the angriest will come first (occasionally last!) Remember where there is one there is usually more than one so continue, go through the whole process again until there is nothing left. When you have finally identified each spirit you will call on their guides to help them to transit as described earlier. Your aim in all clearings is to help the attached spirit not threaten or intimidate them.

It is not your intention to exorcise them, cast them out, punish them, banish them or push them out into the void. This should never be in your mind when you attempt to help them.

Later in the journey when your client has met their team, you will ask them to check your work and carry out any repair work necessary to your client's auric field.

Curses and spells

A curse may behave just like an earthbound spirit or negative entity but it is not as intelligent. A curse may manifest as small negative entities (gargoyle, goblin or small demon like creatures) bothering your client. If you discover a curse during a Crystal Dreaming, track down the perpetrator and find out what is going on. Because the entities carrying out the curse are simple beings all your client has to do is command them:

"Show me you who sent you."

Your client will get a clear picture of the person, who they will know. Once you have done this, we dissolve the curse and call on the perpetrator.

When dealing with the gargoyle like curses your client as two options:

"Thank you for your service, your work is complete; you may go home to light or return from where you came. You no longer have my permission to be here."

Or

"Look inside yourself, what do they see? (Let them tell you).

They will see if they look hard enough a tiny spark, this is their connection to the Divine.

"How does it feel? Good? Let it grow so all of you can feel good."

It will grow and they will be absorbed back into The Source.

Call on the spirit of the person cursing your client and find out why they sent the curse. Your client may need to apologise and ask for forgiveness. The perpetrator may also need to apologise, give the perpetrator a chance to speak and hear them out. Do your best to repair any damage done and settle things amicably. If the perpetrator refuses to co-operate make it clear that anything sent towards your client will be immediately returned to sender with a little extra bonus and leave it at that. You could also point out that this is a free will Universe where we are all sovereign beings. Has this person considered the damage they are doing to their own Karma through such actions?

"Drawing light through the crown, take it down to your power centre or Hara, a hands breadth below the navel in the centre of your body. There build a star pushing out light with every out breath. Allow it to grow filling your body, pushing out shafts of light in every direction, dissolving any energies not totally aligned with light.

When your body is full of light, extend light beyond your body, creating an egg-shape all around you. Allow that to fill with light.

When the egg is complete, see yourself bathing in a cool violet flame, then see a violet flame licking the outside of your egg, leaving a violet hue.

When that feels comfortable create a sparkling gold see-through criss-cross mesh on the outside of the egg and then create a platinum mesh on top of that. You may declare that this mesh will only let love and light in and will repel all other thought forms.

Project a ray of pink from your own heart projecting unconditional love for all things. Allow that to spread out from your heart, forming a bubble that surrounds your whole being.

Now create a mirror ball on the outside of your egg, there should be small spaces between the mirrors which completely cover your egg. Then place a supercharged coating of unconditional love on the mirror which you instruct to reflect any negative intentions back to the sender, along with unconditional love and wishes for enlightenment.

You may now declare out loud,

"I am light,

I am love,

I am protected."

That should ensure anything else sent to the client will be returned to sender. As most people employ amateur witches to curse, the curser will go to her employers asking for more money to resend the curse. After that the whole thing just naturally runs out of steam.

Ancient Egyptian magic

One thing the Ancients, particularly the Egyptians understood and practised well, was magic. You may come across a client who has been dogged with bad luck over many lifetimes. In seeking to discover the source they may recall being punished in ancient Egypt for a serious offence such as abusing a virgin priestess or poisoning another priest or priestess. Chances are they were themselves a member of the elite, a high priest or priestess who abused their power.

What your client may recall is a deliberately painful and drawn out death in which, while they where still conscious, talismans and magical objects were sewn into their partially disembowelled body before they died. In recalling this event your client will become fearful, not just because of the physical and emotional pain, but because they know that the magic placed in their body as punishment will cross time and space and stay with them until it is removed.

You will advise your client to call on the perpetrators and talk to the priests and priestesses involved. Apologies may well be in order. Your client may beg for forgiveness and affirm that centuries later s/he has learned his lesson. Hopefully they will agree, they may want a few promises from your client before they remove them. If they refuse you can ask for a hearing at the Karmic court or your client can remove the talismans themselves.

Demons

Demons may show up in a session. They are all show so do not let your client become terrified of them. They may appear as red eyed, fanged or horned beasts or as a large self aware mass of negative energy. If your client remembers being abused by them in a past life recall and the Demon is not present, to reassure the client, suggest the following affirmation:

> *"You have no power over me, you never have had any power over me, you never will have any power over me. Across time and space as the Universe is my witness, I reclaim my power, I reclaim my freedom.*
>
> *Thank you for your service, thank you for teaching me my limitation. Our agreement is now complete. I have learned all I need to know about fear/despair/anger etc.*
>
> *I now dissolve all agreements with you. I am a being of light, I am a being of love, I am inviolate, I am that I am, I am a free Spirit!*
>
> *So be it."*

If your client encounters a Demon from a past life incident in the present or they realise that it is still attached now, start with the above affirmation. You may then also suggest the Demon look into the centre of their being and tell you what they see there. Remember if it is aggressive to have your client tell it not to be afraid, then have your client say to it several times:

> *"In you I see great light, in you I see great beauty.*
>
> *You are a beautiful being of light, you are loved. You always were loved, you always will be loved.*
>
> *Look inside yourself, to your core, tell me what you see.*
>
> *You are beautiful."*

What happens next can be spectacular. As the Demon looks within it perceives the light that is within us all and it has a profound realisation that it *is* a being of light. In fact it may realise it is an Angel and as the light expands transform into its original form to be greeted by others of its kind.

These beings have been told by their masters that they are not part of the Source or Light and they live in torment. This is a lie as everything is an aspect of the Divine. When they understand that they can merge with light and find peace, which most will do happily.

If they do not wish to look within you can invite the beings who love them unconditionally to join you or ask them to go back from where they came. In any case, however they leave, your client will say as they depart:

"You may not return without my conscious written permission."

Mother Demons

Some will not transform or leave easily when you suggest this as they are fully aware of their past and continue to serve the light, by serving the dark in their role as senior custodians of fear, depression, anger, guilt, etc. These are "Mother" Demons, their service will continue until humanity no longer needs to experience fear based emotions. You will sense their presence in the room as the temperature will drop and you will feel a chill and may start to feel fearful yourself.

You can negotiate with them that they leave your client but you will not be able to persuade them to return to light. You can reclaim your client's power and sovereignty by reminding them that their agreement with your client is complete and your client no longer needs their services. You should be tactful and polite, thanking and honouring them for their service to humanity.

When they do leave, you will remind them that they cannot return without your client's conscious written permission. Expect a visit from that same demon the following evening, it will be checking you out to see if it can teach you more about fear.

Be polite and decline their offer graciously.

The Dark Lord

There is no need to refer to this being by name. In naming him out loud you call him in, so this general term above is both respectful and deliberately vague. This being who is most feared in many cultures, has many names and appearances. He can show up in a Crystal Dreaming session, he may even appear in one of your own lucid dreams as your power and confidence grows. In the twenty-first century he will appear to most westerners as a very slick, charming, urbane and worldly gentleman. He will be well groomed, well dressed, wealthy and apparently friendly.

In your dream he may offer you anything that your heart desires. He will know what this is and will be quite specific in offering it to you - in exchange for signing a piece of paper or contract. DO NOT SIGN!

Your best defence is to have zero attachment to wealth, worldly possessions or success - this gives him no leverage. He understands the laws of the Universe and will back down once contracts are dissolved. He will threaten both you and your clients but if you remain steadfast, clear and cool, he will leave.

In order to create fear in you or your client, he may also appear in his more traditional, terrifying, ancient forms. Either way, remain calm and do not buy into fear when dealing with him.

Ritual abuse

All of the above can be triggered by ritual abuse, memories of which may come up during the release of any entity. Your client may begin to remember horrific abuse by their own family in this lifetime, when releasing the cellular memory related to an attachment or recalling the moment permission was given for the entity to attach.

Recalls of this nature are rare but they can happen during a session.

There are some groups which deliberately abuse children in a ritual space. The fear that the abuse generates creates an energy source for the inter-dimensional beings that the group works with. Abuse may continue for many years and the children themselves may be used for breeding. The child may have been forced or tricked into believing that they took part in human sacrifice or torture. They may have been "married" and forced to have intercourse with a member of the cult channelling or acting, dressed up as the dark lord.

Those who survive are programmed to forget their experiences, which their conscious mind may do, although they remain deeply scarred. The memory is stored in their energy body, waiting to be released when a safe opportunity presents itself. Your Crystal Dreaming session may be that opportunity.

Cases of this nature exist and you may be guided to help a survivor of ritual abuse. You will negotiate with any entity as suggested earlier. The key issues your client will have to deal with are; overcoming their own programmed fear and guilt, breaking any binding agreements with any major negative entity or group and forgiving themselves for participating in the forced ritual abuse of others.

It is appropriate initially that your client call on and forgive the group that abused them:

"I forgive you, I forgive you, I forgive you. With all my heart I freely forgive you.

I forgive you for torturing and abusing me as a child.

In forgiving you I release you from this trauma, as I release myself, to find joy, peace, happiness and freedom. Go in peace, thank you.

We are no longer bound by this trauma. You are released, go in peace."

Then they should call on any non-physical being(s) involved. It is unlikely that any being you are dealing with at this level of abuse will accept your offer for them to transit home to light, but you must always offer. What is most likely is that your client will need to reclaim their power by facing their deepest fear (eg. the entity they may have been forced to marry), telling them their agreement is complete, thanking them for their learning experience and giving them permission to leave.

Even the most threatening, malevolent or apparently powerful beings cannot stay without your client's permission. It is your clients remaining fear that gives them a toehold. Your role is to support your client's compassion for themselves and any attached being. Remember that love is repulsive to them, they will leave if you can support your client's empowerment and help lift their vibration:

"I call on the being I was forced to marry, I call on the being who raped me, please stand before me now.

All agreements between us are now dissolved. You have no power over me, you never have had any power over me, you never will have any power over me.

Thank you for teaching me my limitations, I forgive you for abusing me. Our relationship is complete. Go in peace, you are now released from all agreements. They no longer bind us. Be at peace.

You may not return without my conscious written permission."

You will feel its presence, be calm and resolute. Beings operating at this level are unlikely to return to light as they are fulfilling their chosen role in service to dark. Treat them with respect, be courteous and firm, honour their choices, do not be intimidated by them and they will leave.

In the case of a ritual marriage, you may also use this affirmation:

"The ritual marriage I was forced into was not entered into with my free will and cannot therefore be binding. I dissolve all vows I made under duress, now. The agreement we entered into is null and void and no longer binds us. I am a free spirit, so be it. Go in peace."

If you reach an impasse, which is unlikely, suggest your client request a hearing in the Karmic court. Find out what is happening and why and plead for clemency or a release of Karma.

Cleansing yourself after a healing

After your client has departed, centre yourself, do the cleansing exercises you already know. If you are a pranic healer or Reiki channel, sweep or scan your whole body using white prana paying particular attention to the head, nape of neck and solar plexus. If you have the slightest doubt about your own state of well being, have a hot Epsom salts bath. Fully immerse your body and shower after that. You could take several drops of mountain penny royal and/or dissolve them into a hot bath too, use Aura Soma or any other cleansing and purification method that works for you.

Always have an agreement with another responsible healer (preferably a Crystal Dreaming practitioner) who understands your work, that they will respond to any urgent request for a healing from you at any time.

Danger signs for you

If you choose to pursue clearing or find yourself presented with it, then at some stage you are likely to slip up and find yourself with an attached spirit. Be aware that this can and does happen even to the most experienced healer. Observe yourself in the hours and days after a healing. You should be looking after yourself, so you should notice any imbalance in your own systems quickly.

Things to look out for are; any kind of irrational fear about anything, uneasiness, depression, grouchiness and murderous or suicidal thoughts. The antidote to fear and anger is joy and love so if you find yourself suffering from these symptoms treat yourself to a trip to the cinema or lots of the funniest videos you can find. Watch one a day at least until the feelings disperse. There is no space for fear when you are laughing and giggling. If you are blessed with a loving family, express your love for them openly and joyfully. Be affectionate and playful every day all day, surround yourself with love.

Love is a vibration that is repulsive to those who are not aligned with it. It is also the most powerful force in the Universe, so use it! Create a still and focused place where you can connect with the Divine. Invite the beings who love you unconditionally to help in cleansing and purifying your aura.

Do the cleansing exercise twice daily. For added protection perceive liquid gold running down the nape of your neck to the base of your spine. Declare out loud:

"I am light, I am love, I am protected."

If you find yourself suffering from a severe headache, irrational fear or becoming nauseous during this exercise, or when you yourself state the clearing affirmations mentioned earlier, then it is time for you to see another healer. Call the healer you have an agreement with immediately, *do not hesitate.* Your energy is depleted and is being further depleted, it is better if you call on assistance and use someone else's fresh energy to help you out. Do not hesitate or doubt your own feelings, the longer it is there the harder it is to remove, so do not hesitate or doubt your own feelings.

Conclusion

Your own well-being is paramount. If you are not well and whole how can you possibly be of service to others and our beautiful planet?

Look after yourself.

Remember that the beings that you will help may appear fierce or angry, these emotions are manifestations of fear. Consider the most aggressive entities you encounter to be like self-willed children having a tantrum, they have temporarily 'lost the plot' and if you are firm and loving with them, they will settle down. You must *never* allow yourself to become angry or intimidated by them; be firm, be patient and be loving. The power of unconditional love overcomes all challenges.

NEVER, EVER, ALLOW YOURSELF TO BECOME FEARFUL.

At all times, remember that you are dealing with another aspect of the Divine, another aspect of All There Is *and therefore another aspect of yourself.* Be compassionate. All beings everywhere are part of the same source of love and light. All beings in their very core have a spark of Divine energy which is love itself, like us they lose touch with that sometimes. For many lifetimes or even eons, a being may become so separated from the Source that it will convince itself it is no longer a being of light.

All beings everywhere are living aspects of love and light.

You can help them, remember this. You can be tough if you need to be but you must be loving, as you are dealing with a long lost brother or sister who is ready to come home and find peace.

Always work with love in your heart
EXPECT THE UNEXPECTED!

101

Chapter 12
Empowering your client

The primary objective of all Crystal Dreaming sessions is your client's conscious re-connection with absolute bliss through their own higher guidance or spiritual team; their guides, teachers and friends, the beings who love them unconditionally.

Once with their team, having followed the correct protocols and checked their authenticity you can enjoy expanding your clients consciousness and empowering them. You will be privileged to facilitate major positive shifts for your clients that are awesomely powerful and life transforming. You will always be guided by your own intuition. I offer a few suggestions to help you along your way, you would not normally attempt all of the following in one session!

Dissolving pre-birth agreements

There are a number of secret and not so secret societies operating on this planet now. If either of your client's parents, particularly the father, has been a member of a guild, lodge or group that meets in secret and carries out rituals of any sort it is advisable that you suggest the following affirmation to your client. It seems that parents are able to make promises and agreements on their children's behalf before they are born. There is no harm in clearing the air and reclaiming our sovereignty:

> *"As the universe is my witness, I _____ of my own free will now dissolve any agreements with any secret society, circle, guild, lodge or group that is not for my Divine highest good, made on my behalf before I was born. I revoke all past life contracts that are not part of my Divine plan or totally aligned with light and unconditional love. There never has been, is, and never will be, any organization, group, circle, guild or secret society that has power over me or my lineage. I reclaim my freedom, I AM A FREE SPIRIT! So be it."*

We may also ourselves have been a member of a coven, guild or society in past lives and made contracts with them that are not focused on our divine highest good now. It is appropriate that your client dissolve agreements with these groups too. They are still binding until dissolved, whether made of your own free will or not:

> *As the universe is my witness, I _____ of my own free will now dissolve any and all agreements with any secret society, circle, guild, lodge or group that is not for my Divine highest good, that I may have made myself in a previous life. There never has been, is, and*

never will be, any organization, group, circle, guild or secret society that has power over me or my lineage. I reclaim my freedom, I reclaim my power. I AM A FREE SPIRIT! So be it."

Reclaiming past life skills

It is a good idea to suggest that your clients team show them any past life skills that may be relevant to their mission in this life. Having seen what they are capable of they may make the following affirmation. This affirmation will not only be useful for your client in any Crystal Dreaming journey, but for yourself to affirm daily in front of a mirror each morning:

"I _____ of my own free will and in full consciousness, across time and space, as the Universe is my witness now reclaim my power. I reclaim all that I am; I reclaim all of the abilities that I have developed in past lives. I command that they manifest in this body NOW.

I now release any promises I may have made with myself that limit the use of my power. I am ready to step into my power and dedicate every cell of my being to using this knowledge and abilities in service to light and in service to love for the Divine highest good of all. NOW!"

These skills may not manifest in the conscious mind but will rather be felt as strong intuition or knowing, after the session.

I am a free spirit

A great affirmation for you or your client to make any time, particularly if they wish to reclaim their power and sovereignty:

"As the Universe is my witness, I declare now, I am a free Spirit, I am a sovereign being of light.

Beray sheet ehyeh asher ehyer, Beray sheet ehyeh asher ehyer, Beray sheet ehyeh asher ehyer.

I am that I am, I am a being of free will, I am a free spirit, so be it!"

The repeated affirmation is in Hebrew and many believe it is one of the most powerful we can speak.

Accessing your blueprint or divine plan

We all have a blueprint or divine plan we draw up before we incarnate here. We frequently become distracted from it and forget our life's purpose. Having reunited your client with their team ask for their teams support as you make this affirmation together:

"As the Universe is my witness, I_____ of my own free will, reclaim my awareness of the Divine, I am an aspect of God, I acknowledge the god within, the GOD I AM.

I now ask that my own Divine plan or blueprint be brought into alignment, that I be made aware of any actions I need to take on this plane to fulfil that plan, NOW.

I ask this of my own free will, in full consciousness and for my own Divine highest good, so be it."

Your client may find thoughts, feelings or pictures coming into their consciousness as they speak, they may have a more spectacular experience! Any actions impelled from the Divine will *always* be positive. You may further strengthen this affirmation with:

"As the Universe is my witness, I_____ now accept my destiny. I accept that I am an aspect of the Divine, I accept that as such I AM THAT I AM.

I freely declare that I am now ready to step into my own power and the fullness of my being, in service to humanity, in service to light, in service to love and the Divine plan. It is my choice as a free spirit to explore my own potential, and I offer myself in service to Light and unconditional love, now and always. So be it."

Downloading Light codes

You may also request, if it is appropriate as part of your client's Divine plan, that their light codes be downloaded. These codes are not stored in your client's cellular memory and are implanted on request. Your client is in an appropriate space to do this:

"Of my own free will, I _____ request a downloading of light codes, relating to my mission here on Earth, into every cell of my being, NOW!"

The codes will enter your client as streams of glyphs or coded light. They will not understand the content of the download consciously, but it will affect their abilities in relation to their mission here. Once downloaded, these codes will be activated by key events in your clients life.

In activating a client during a session there may be a physical response, your client's body my shake and vibrate uncontrollably, suggest they breathe into the experience and surrender to it. If it becomes too intense your client can ask their team to reduce the volume of the information they are downloading.

Activating the twelve strand DNA

Our scientists presently believe that a large proportion of our DNA is "junk" because they do not understand its purpose. In any Crystal Dreaming session you may activate this twelve strand DNA:

"Across time and space, I choose to activate my 12 strand DNA, I ask my own team to assist with this process NOW!"

Twelve strand DNA activation may increase your clients psychic abilities and sensitivity to their team and subtle energies. I suspect it does much more. You may witness a similar physical reaction to that mentioned above although this is less common with DNA activation.

I am loved

If your client is feeling sad or lonely or confused after a release then this is an affirmation that will help:

"I am loved. All my needs are met. Everything is as it should be. Challenges I do not understand now, I will in due course. I start this day with love in my heart for all creation, I love my family, my friends and my community. I love myself. I am a beautiful living aspect of the Divine. So be it."

Abundance

You may find some clients who are under the illusion that having a spiritually aware and active life means poverty and lack of wealth:

"I am surrounded by abundance. All my needs are met. I am continually provided for by the Divine. I now claim all that is mine by Divine birthright. Material wealth flows to me effortlessly. I profitably and joyfully work for Spirit as I fulfil my part in the Divine plan.

I now dissolve all vows of poverty (and chastity too, if you wish) I have made in past lives. I no longer need to experience poverty, I have learned all I need to know about lack of abundance on the material plane. I accept joy, peace, freedom and material abundance into my life NOW."

Many of us have been on a spiritual path for many lifetimes and many will have made binding vows of chastity and poverty in the past, until we dissolve them they still have power. Wealth need not control us, it can be a great tool to help us achieve our goals here on Earth. Have your client make this affirmation with all their heart, with selfless motivation and they may be pleasantly surprised by the results.

Dissolving negative programming

We are exposed to massive amounts of fear based programming through the mass media every day. Whilst it may be wise to be up to date on global developments, this programming affects us, sometimes subtly sometimes profoundly. It is created deliberately and it is worth taking the time to undo its influence. Your client may repeat the following affirmation:

"As the Universe is my witness I _____ of my own free will, now dissolve all fear based attachments created by the mass media. They no longer have power over me and I reject them. I choose now to focus on love for this planet, love for this place, love for my community, love for my family and friends and love for myself. Goodbye media influence, goodbye amplified fear and artificial limitations. Hello Fun, Hello Joy, HELLO FREEDOM! I choose to separate myself from media control, NOW!"

The great invocation

Channelled some years ago this remains a very powerful affirmation for you and your client to do together. Invoke the appropriate Master for your client's spiritual beliefs and cultural background in line six:

"From the point of light within the mind of God
Let light stream forth into the minds of all
Let light descend on Earth.
From the point of love within the heart of God
Let love stream forth into the hearts of all
May Christ (or another appropriate Master) return to Earth
From the centre where the will of God is known
Let purpose guide the little wills of all
The purpose which the Masters know and serve.
From the centre which we call humanity
Let the plan of Love and Light work out
May it seal the door where evil dwells.
Let Light, Love and Power restore the Plan on Earth.
I am one with the Ascended Masters of Light
I am one with the Cosmic Light Command
I am one with the Angelic Light Force
I am one with Love and Light Divine
I am at peace with all Humanity
Now there is peace in my heart
There is peace everywhere
I am that which I am - a shining light for all. I am that I am."

Calling on Guides and Masters

Sometimes if your client's guides do not show up spontaneously you may suggest they call on them. Preferably they will discover them themselves.

"I _____ of my own free will, now call on my spirit guides, teachers and friends, I ask you to surround me with your love and light. I now humbly and respectfully call on the Ascended Master closest to my heart. Please enter my consciousness now and show yourself to me."

Most Masters are obviously human and loving, however there is one individual, Dr. Lorfan, a Master healer, who appears as a praying mantis. Follow the usual protocols and do not be alarmed if your clients describe him as praying mantis like. He is a great healer with, I suspect, a great sense of humour.

Merging with the Higher Self

Your client having met and worked with their guides may wish to meet their Higher Self and ask for a merging with them. This is usually an awesome experience because as they become one, your client will enter a state of peace and bliss:

" I live within the light, I love within the light, I laugh within the light, I am sustained by the light, I joyously serve the light. For I AM the light, I AM the light, I AM the light.

I am, I am, I am.

I am an aspect of the Divine, I am an infinite being of light, I am an infinite being of love, I am aware of my Higher Self.

I am that I am. I am that I am. I am that I am.

I now request a merging with my Higher Self."

In the state of oneness that follows a merging you may suggest that they explore how far their consciousness reaches. They will be surprised to find it touches everything, everywhere. The Higher Self exists as a star in space. From that point it can also be a powerful experience to look back at this beautiful planet and also look at their life's journey here. This can put any apparently insurmountable challenges in perspective. If a person has been experiencing fear you can ask them how it feels to be one with their Higher Self (who does not experience fear and is in a constant state of bliss). The Higher Self can also offer guidance on your clients progress through life and their life plan.

Your client as High Priest or Priestess

Many light-workers and healers are treading again the ancient path of healing and shamanism as a high priest or priestess in service to the Divine plan. Occasionally you will have the privilege of activating a dormant priest or priestess.

After consulting with your client's team as to its appropriateness you can suggest that they make the following affirmation:

"As the Universe is my witness, I _____ with love in my heart and for the Divine highest good of all, now command my body to release any cellular memory that will attest to any past life experience as an initiate of a mystery school, high priest, priestess, shaman or healer.

I freely accept the consequences of knowing who I am and I dedicate myself to using my past life experience for the benefit of all. I now release any blocks I may have placed for my own protection, I dissolve any promises I may have made with myself that limit the use of my power. I am ready to serve the Divine plan, I release this memory into full awareness. I call on the High Priest/ Priestess I am, step forward NOW!"

Suggest your client ask to be shown what they achieved in that role and how they can harness its power in the 21st century.

Atlantis

The Atlanteans lived on this Earth between about 32,000 and 11,000 years ago. They were a technologically advanced race that may have been the result of interbreeding between human women and advanced humanoid extraterrestrials. Such strands of humanity are referred to as "Star seeded."

Atlanteans were masters of crystal technology and many crystal healers operating now are reincarnations of past masters. They are here to make recompense for the enormous damage they did to humanity by abusing their powers in Atlantis. Atlanteans were able to harness energy through crystals, controlling their atmosphere, performing surgery and manipulating objects in space. In their desire to experiment with nature and exert their power, they became reckless and created their own downfall. You can ask for your client to be shown the Atlantean story and their part in it, if it is appropriate.

It appears in the later stages of their society, as it crumbled into decadence, there was a desire in the Atlantean hierarchy to have power over a more peace loving race Lemurians. It is possible a deliberate attack on Lemuria turned into a huge natural disaster or that experiments with hydrogen or heavy water created a disastrous chain reaction. The Atlantean power lust triggered the destruction of their own continent and civilisation. It was inundated during the Great Flood referred to in The Bible.

Prior to the destruction of Atlantis, colonies existed in Egypt, North America and South America. The Maya, North American Indian and the Ancient Egyptians all have an Atlantean heritage and transferred some Atlantean crystal techniques and practices into their cultures. I believe the Native American knowledge and use of crystals for shamanic journeys and healing has its roots in Atlantis.

Those past life Atlanteans in bodies here now will have a particular affinity with Aquamarine and green obsidian. You may trigger an Atlantean recall by placing Aquamarine pyramids on the throat, heart and third eye chakras. Many Atlanteans were crystal Masters so if your client has an affinity with crystals the following request to your client's team may be a useful experience:

> "Beloved friends, provided it be for my divine highest good, please take me back to Atlantis, now."

Asking for a clear description of the places they visit and the technologies used there can be very enlightening. They will no doubt meet friends and others who are also incarnated now.

Ancient Egypt

Clients drawn to healing may well have been healers in past lives and will probably have learnt some of their craft in Ancient Egypt. You can trigger a recall by placing Lapis pyramids on the throat, heart and third eye chakras. The Ancient Egyptians were master magicians, so be aware if you journey there. Your client should hold their guides' hands as they explore.

> "Beloved friends, provided it be for my divine highest good, please take me back to Ancient Egypt, now."

If they decide to explore any pyramids or temples the following affirmation should be used:

> "I enter this place, with love in my heart, and for my own Divine highest good. I honour my forefathers, the builders of this great temple, and humbly request their permission to enter this sacred place, now. I come in peace."

Wait for a positive response. I do not advise your client to open any sarcophagi or tombs unless they are advised to do so by their own team. If they interact with any of the Ancient gods proceed with caution, they may not love your client unconditionally.

I recommend further research into the culture of Ancient Egypt.

ET Guides

Occasionally you may find an Extraterrestrial guide, usually with those who have incarnated here for the first time, or who have an ET connection from a, sometimes distant, past life. In this situation always ask the appropriate "Do you love me unconditionally?" questions before proceeding further.

Using open ended questions, obtain a description of the ET. Loving ETs do radiate light and love and it should be tangible. Those with very strong ET connections may be here as passive observers and their lives will be being monitored by their friends back home who are usually positive beings, intrigued by planet Earth and committed not to interfere in our affairs.

Homesickness and going home

Most people with ET connections may not be terribly surprised to discover them, possibly having never felt truly at home here. It is possible for your client to be taken back to their planet of origin if they wish. Working with their team they may make the following affirmation:

"Beloved friends, provided it be for my divine highest good, please take me to my home planet now. I promise to return to this body when asked to do so."

Be prepared for an outpouring of deep emotional feelings of homesickness. They may not have been home for some time, they may even have become lost due to some mishap.

Volunteers from other parts of the Universe have incarnated here to assist in our transition into light as a species. Their role is to hold the vibration of love while they are here. These pure beings have found it hard to be here from the beginning, the fear based density of life on this planet is confusing and painful for them. They may have tried to escape through suicide or drugs. Be sure to ask their team what their mission is here and if necessary, remind them that they came as a volunteer and their mission is not yet complete.

Be aware that after a session like this your client may become depressed. This will pass if they continue to focus on their mission and know that in due course they will be reunited with their "Star family."

Channelling Higher Beings

Channelling involves another being takes over your client's body completely, a benign possession. This occasionally happens spontaneously during a session; take the following precautions before you allow this to happen.

Find out as much as you can about the being who wishes to speak through your client. Does s/he love your client unconditionally? Why do they wish to speak through your client? Is it because of a previous agreement? Find out more, this agreement may not now be for your client's Divine highest good. Proceed with caution.

If you, your client and their team all agree that it is appropriate that a channelling happen, ask for the following assurances: that the being loves your client unconditionally; that the channelling will be for a limited specified time, after which your client will be returned to their body; that the being agrees to monitor all the bodily functions of your client ensuring their physical well-being; that the being agrees to leave your client's body reinstating your client's consciousness should you request it at any time.

There will be some vocal and physical adjustment as the being first speaks, they have access to your clients language and vocabulary. Your client is likely to detox after their first experience. They have embodied a high vibrational energy. Even if you request your client return to their body in good health and energised, they are likely to be tired afterwards and may go through a minor healing crisis in the following days.

Whilst out of their body your client may be taken elsewhere or may observe the whole experience from the outside, they are unlikely to remember what was said during the channelling, unless you request it.

Light quotient

A great thing for anyone on a spiritual path is to increase the level of Light and Love in their being.

> *"Please raise the light quotient in every cell of my being to the maximum I can sustain."*

Akashic records

Your client may request a visit the Akashic library. There they can view their own Akashic records, their entire experience as a sentient being from oneness to individuated consciousness.

They will usually be met by a helpful librarian who may appear as a bald headed bespectacled man who will guide them through the library.

Returning to the Source

A great way to finish any session is to request that your client be returned to the Source of all Light and Love and bathe in that energy for a short while. Asking their team to help they may say:

> *"Of my own free will, I _____ request a merging with*

the source of all Light and Love. Please take me home, I am ready to experience oneness with All There Is, NOW!"

This can be a profound experience for your client, give them the space to enjoy it. It is not unusual for people to cry with the level of joy they experience.

Conclusion

Understanding the incredible level of empowerment that you may facilitate for your clients gives an insight as to why fear based beings will try hard to block or disrupt a session. All obstacles may be overcome providing you believe it to be possible and pass this firm belief on to your client. Remember...

Be clear in your intentions
Anger is a manifestation of fear
Knowledge is power
Forgiveness equals freedom

We are ALL extraordinarily powerful
We ARE limitless beings of light and love

Case studies

I include some accounts of healings for your consideration. The following offer a good overview of the types of situation you may encounter as your work with Crystal Dreaming progresses. Refer to my book "Diary of an Urban Shaman" for further in depth case studies.

Fear of the dark

"Helena" is a mature, aristocratic-looking woman who has come to see me to find out why a childhood fear of the dark still haunts her. Prior to our session commencing I ask some questions in order to understand what I might be dealing with. Phobias may relate to childhood trauma, so I ask what kind of place she grew up in. In a soft European accent she replies: "In a castle, with dungeons."

Her family had lived in an old European castle for most of her childhood and she had spent many hours playing in the rooms, grounds and dungeons, where once, as a little girl she had become very frightened. I proceed with the session guiding Helena into an altered state where she has a total recall of her childhood experience. She can clearly see herself as a child playing in the castle dungeons.

She can also see what she could not clearly perceive as a child; that close to her is the tortured soul of an earthbound spirit. A man who, centuries earlier, was locked up in the dark, tortured and left to die a lonely and painful death underneath her family home. As a child she senses his presence, becomes frightened and calls out for help. This gives the earthbound spirit permission to help by attaching himself to her, until this session. Her own childhood fear of the dark was being amplified by the terror of his own experience. In such a case it is relatively easy, once the client becomes aware of the situation, to counsel the spirit and assist him on his journey home to light.

After thanking and forgiving the earthbound spirit, Helena's fear of the dark leaves with him. The session finishes with a reunion with her own spirit guides, who had been unable to communicate clearly with her because of the Earthbound spirit's presence. They take her to a place of such exquisite beauty and love that Helena becomes ecstatic. Not since she had been in an accident years previously, and been clinically dead for a short period, had she experienced such bliss.

After years of being unable to sleep in the dark she can now switch off all her house lights, step onto her balcony and enjoy the spectacular view she has of the night lights of the city she lives in.

Inability to be intimate

"Angela" was a mature teacher who was unable to strike-up and maintain intimate relationships. Because of an obvious attraction to crystals and an intuitive feel for their properties she decided to experience a Crystal Dreaming session to find out why she was so drawn to them. I expected her to discover a past life experience as a crystal healer or priestess, but we did not get that far. During the session we discovered an irate female spirit attached to her. This woman was a jealous past life sister who did not want Angela to have any other intimate relationships.

My aim was to find out more about their relationship and the circumstances of her death so I could counsel her and persuade her to leave, but I did not get to do that either. Angela, sensing where my questions where leading refused point blank to allow her sister to leave claiming that they loved each other and that they supported each other now and always. I agreed that it was entirely Angela's decision and closed the session with the earthbound spirit still attached, one of the few cases where a client refused to release the attached spirit. Angela's relationship challenges continue.

Irrational fear

"Susan" was in her mid thirties and a successful Sydney executive. For no apparent reason she found herself suffering from intense and irrational fears, suicidal thoughts and deep depression. Having tried conventional psychiatry and medicine, to no avail, she turned to the alternative of Crystal Dreaming and was referred to me. As this sounded like a case of possession I chose to work with one of the mediums I had been training.

The woman's apartment was well ordered and tidy, she was smartly dressed but obviously nervous. I chose not to take Susan into an altered state with crystals, because as she was fearful she would not have been a good subject. Also, if what I suspected was correct, the experience would be very intense for her. We proceeded by putting the medium in an altered state. Sure enough, after some games of hide and seek and playing the demon, we discovered a very angry deceased black magician. He was having a ball driving this woman (amongst others) to distraction. He was thriving on the energy her fear was generating. After some negotiation and a few offers of alternative courses of action, I persuaded him to accept the assistance of his own guides and to go home to light. He was very fearful of retribution when he reached the higher dimensions. I was able to truthfully reassure him that there would be no retribution there.

What I did not say was that in due course after rest and rehabilitation his spirit would be given the opportunity to return to Earth and continue its journey of evolution here. Part of that journey will be to experience all the pain and fear he has caused for others. When he does return he will be ready for that experience.

In cases of possession it is rare for there to be only one spirit present. We then discovered a teenage girl who had been abducted, raped, strangled and left to die in a ditch by a truck driver. She was lost and confused and just needed to tell her story. We helped her home to light. We found several more lost souls and were able to assist them in their passage home to light. By the end of the evening Susan was clear and free of fear and spirit attachments. We then introduced her to her spirit guides.

Her guides informed us that the attachments began after Susan had a skiing accident several years ago, when in a great deal of pain she became weak and vulnerable and begged for assistance in easing her pain. Thus unintentionally giving our deceased magician permission to attach and make mischief.

I gave Susan an exercise to do every day for the rest of her life. She said that she was not prepared to accept what had happened as it was beyond her belief system. I said fair enough, but asked her to let me know how she felt in two weeks. Two weeks later she told me she had never felt better. She now lives a completely normal life and does her psychic protection exercises morning and evening.

Compulsive behaviour

"Cheryl" is in her mid-thirties and is a professional nurse. In her session we discover an earthbound spirit had been with her since childhood. After a childhood trauma, Cheryl (as a child) had begged the Universe for help, creating an opportunity for the spirit to attach itself to her. In this case, it was a misguided male spirit who had frightened the woman since her childhood in dreams and visions. After a little resistance he was persuaded to go home to light. We also discovered the spirit of this woman's aborted child who was so keen to enter her family that he had stuck around after the termination. It was an emotional departure but the spirit of the child left willingly enough after being assured it was loved very much.

Some time after the session Cheryl approached me and confided that since the session the dreams had ceased, but also that a childhood compulsion to masturbate had also left with the spirit. This was his way of entertaining himself whilst he was attached to her.

Intense and unpredictable anger

In another case I received calls from several local crystal shops regarding a lady in her mid forties who they had recommended see me, as they suspected she was possessed. She then called me, obviously distressed and confused.

When this slightly built woman arrived, we went straight into a session. As soon as I had placed her in an altered state, an extremely angry male with a loud deep voice started speaking through her in Afrikaans, whilst trying to strangle me with her small but surprisingly strong hands.

As I do not speak Afrikaans I tried to get him to speak in English. He started abusing me in broken English, but I persuaded him to tell his story. He was an Afrikaner miner of mixed race who was trapped in a cave-in and left for dead by his mates. He died a horribly slow and painful death in the dark. He had attached to the client after she had a childhood bicycle accident and ever since had forced her into fits of violent rage that had lead to an A.V.O. being placed on her when she almost bit her husband's finger off.

The Afrikaner's route home was provided by his wife and children who I called in from the spirit realm. You did not have to speak Afrikaans to understand his feelings when he was reunited with them, it was a very emotional reunion. He left peacefully. Since that session the client's mood swings have ceased and she leads a normal life.

Stubborn and mysterious illness

"Pamela" drove 900 kilometres to see me as a last desperate attempt to heal herself. After four years of misery, apparently allergic to everything and easily exhausted, she was debilitated by aches and pains, had low energy, was sensitive to electrical power, suffered from bouts of nausea and intense migraines. All this after surviving two marriages in which she was physically abused and threatened.

She knew her challenge could not be solved by conventional medicine and told me she had spent over $10,000 on a range of alternative and traditional therapies, none of which had permanently relieved her condition. Her session was the first time she had consulted a crystal healer who could assist her to move between worlds, access the spirit realm, diagnose and treat the issue herself.

One session uncovered the key to her challenges. She finds herself witnessing, then reliving a past life trauma. She sees a man with a violent temper become insanely jealous of his beautiful, vivacious wife. He beats her repeatedly then eventually completely loses all self control and strangles her to death.

I am aware of what she is witnessing but she is not. I suggest she feel the vibration of those in the scene and see if she recognises anyone. She does and the penny drops, she realises that she is the abusive male and is stricken with remorse. Even though she is a woman now she still loves her wife of that time very much. We call on the spirit of the abused wife and counsel them both. It is a very emotional reunion, after some tears the wife forgives my client and absolves her of her Karmic debt. I ensure this is verified by a higher authority and it is confirmed her Karma is played out, level and complete. She does not have to suffer any more, she does not have to endure the pain she chose before she was born.

All the major physical manifestations of disease disappeared during that session. Pamela had no problem accepting the truth of her experience because of the depth of emotion she felt during the session. She now leads a normal and happy life.

Karma

On releasing the cellular memory "Janet" observes an intriguing re-run of an incident she is not involved with. She observes three Ancient Roman senators meeting over what appear to be plans to a city. A fourth man enters dressed in green and stabs one of the senators to death. Janet can not identify herself in this scene and when she asks was she the murderer she is told "You may as well have been." We deduce that she must have hired the murderer. We call on the spirit of the murdered man, he confirms that is what happened. Janet prostrates herself and begs forgiveness, she is forgiven, and she asks is the debt now lifted? No it is not and it is out of this spirit's control to do so.

In this kind of situation I advise my client that she needs to ask for a hearing at a Karmic court and that she should treat the court with respect. The court goes into discussion and asks questions. I act as a barrister, helping her plead their case for the permanent release of their Karma.

In this case they heard our case and responded. The court was not prepared to lift the Karma. We asked why and the client was shown that the spirit in question had reincarnated as an ex-lover of the client and that she had done further damage to him on this plane by the way in which they had parted. She vowed to make amends and contact the man on this plane and beg forgiveness in person, on this condition the karma was lifted.

Janet confided in me after the session that her present life relationship with this man had always been stormy and whilst attracted to her he always seemed to be angry with her. Now we know why. Prior to the session she had been aware of a 'stuckness' in her life she just couldn't put her finger on, that feeling disappeared after the session.

What is interesting about this particular case is that although she travelled halfway around the world to meet him in person and beg his forgiveness, she was unable to actually follow through and say it, in person.

Mary's recurring nightmares

"Mary" had always had disturbing dreams and was prone to feeling fearful and helpless. During her session she had a graphic recall of a past life sacrifice that was not voluntary and brought up feelings of absolute terror. In this situation the client knew she was drugged, her throat had been slit and she was bleeding to death. A half-human half-beast was drinking her blood and raping her as she died.

The key here is for Mary to confront the feelings of fear and helplessness that had permeated every life since then. This she did by staring the beast in the face and saying:

> *"You have no power over me, you never have had any power over me nor will you ever have any power over me Across Time and Space as the Universe is my witness, I break all ties with you.*
>
> *I am a being of light, I am a being of love, I am inviolate, I AM THAT I AM, I am a free Spirit! So be it."*

The memory of the incident ceased to have any power over her and her life is changed for the better.

Brad's recurring nightmares

"Brad" was an all round sportsman and jogger, he looked after himself and was studying sports massage. Whilst on a weekend retreat with other practitioners he found himself night after night falling out of bed screaming, desperately trying to get out of the room, disturbing everyone in the process. His Higher Self was preparing him to release a past life trauma which he did in his session. Prior to the session he told me that all he could remember of his dream was that he was in an engine room in what he thought was a German WW2 battleship. He thought perhaps he needed to get out because the ship was sinking.

What we discovered was that he was in the engine room of the battleship but that he suffered a violent disagreement about money with his mate who had struck a fatal blow to Brad's head with a huge spanner. As he died all he wanted to do was get into the fresh air and leave the engine room, which he failed to do.

Apart from forgiving his murderer, what we really needed to do was complete the death by allowing his traumatised spirit to leave the engine room and get some fresh air. This we did and the nightmares ceased.

Tennis Elbow

"Fran" a therapist herself, wishes to understand why she has a persistent health challenge in her left elbow. She has had surgery to try and relieve the constant nagging pain that emanates from this point with no success. She perceives several things on her journey. She is holding on to negative energy at this point in her body and she has a reluctance to ask for help herself when she needs it. After releasing this energy and the pain associated with it we discover why energy is collecting at this point in her body.

Fran relives an incident from a past life in which she is a powerful male warrior. She is in hand to hand combat when her opponent inflicts a fatal wound by slicing her arm off just above the elbow. The pain and anger she feels as her opponent finishes her off is immense and it imprints on her consciousness until now.

We resolve the situation by forgiving her opponent and expressing gratitude for the learning that this experience has given her. The pain disappears immediately and permanently.

(An interesting thing about this recall was that both she and her opponent were not from this planet.)

Low self esteem

In exploring why "Sara" had feelings of low self esteem and self worth, despite being a vibrant and talented individual, we explored her past life experience. A scene slowly unfolds leading to the realisation that she was spread-eagled on a sacrificial slab inside what appears to be an Inca or Aztec pyramid. She knows she is about to be cut open and sacrificed and is terrified. We discover that she was there of her own free will. She is drugged and cannot feel any pain. As we access the memory of that life, she realises she has been trained since childhood for this moment. She is an honoured volunteer, a vestal virgin or priestess whose voluntary death will benefit her community immeasurably.

At the moment of death her spirit was to leave her body and create a protective energetic umbrella over her people until the next sacrifice. In fact, she had collapsed into her own terror, despite her years of training. This meant that she died an undignified and fearful death, holding her spirit in and not fulfilling her chosen role. This disappointed her community and the priestesses who had trained her.

To resolve this issue, she went through the sacrifice again, this time following her training and surrendering to the process, dying, without fear. The waves of gratitude that swept through the room were tangible and deeply moving. Issue resolved... self esteem restored.

Anger and Despair

"Fiona" a mature businesswoman, seeks to understand why despite having a successful career and family life, she feels an undercurrent of anger and despair.

During her session she starts feeling very cold and shivery. Her teeth are chattering and her feet feel like there are shards of glass in them. She is shaking that much that I need to place a blanket over her and try to warm her up. She is in the snow dying. She has been an Innuit or Eskimo wise woman and healer, loved and respected by her community. She is now old and cannot keep up with her clan as they move camp. She has been left behind in the snow to die and she is not feeling very happy about it. How could they leave her to die when she had given so much to her community?

This situation is resolved by her comforting her past life self and explaining that it is time for her to leave her body peacefully without anger or resentment. Fiona comforts this woman as she dies and she leaves her body in peace. At this point Fiona's anger and resentment leave her too.

Nagging throat challenge

"Shaun" is a successful young fashion designer who had a mysterious and continuing throat problem. He constantly felt that his throat was blocked, and found himself swallowing hard and clearing his throat, particularly if he was under any kind of pressure.

Accessing the Time-Space matrix via Crystal Dreaming we navigate a route through his previous lives and find ourselves at a time and place where he is in a chariot race against his best mate. They are racing in a stadium in front of a huge crowd. Whoever wins the race will live, the loser be disgraced and publicly executed. There are no rules in this race and Shaun has mixed emotions, a man he loves is racing against him for his life. As the chariots take a corner and push against each other his friend leans over and executes a swift backhand cut with a sword almost completely decapitating Shaun. His head is severed at the throat falling back, attached to the rest of his body only by his spinal chord.

Shaun dies feeling betrayed and distraught that his best mate, of all people, could do this to him. Shaun relives the experience forgiving his friend and affirming he has not been betrayed and all is in perfect order. His throat condition disappears during the session.

Sensitive to being touched

"Bob" is an accountant who since birth has been very sensitive to being touched in the abdominal area. This was constraining intimate relationships; he wished to understand why this condition which had perplexed doctors and family was happening.

Crystal Dreaming took Bob back to his most recent past life, which turned out to have a traumatic ending. Almost immediately Bob was writhing in agony holding his stomach, he was badly wounded and frightened. He knew he was about to die. As he was in such distress we stepped out of his body and observed the scene unfolding from the outside.

What we witnessed was a group of Aussie diggers in the Second World War, in or close to a jungle. Bob had been hit and was surrounded by his mates, who were doing their best to ease his discomfort. His platoon were ordered to make another sortie into the jungle, his mates left him, reluctantly obeying orders, knowing he would die a lonely and painful death whilst they were away.

Bob was now witnessing his own death and it was not pleasant. He could see that his soldier self was frightened and alone. I suggested that he approach the dying soldier and see if the soldier could see him, he could. I suggested that he take the soldier in his arms and reassure him, explaining to him that he was his future self and that he need not fear as he was not alone and his consciousness would live on after his body died.

The soldier died peacefully in Bob's arms, a very moving experience for both Bob and myself. Before we left the scene, I suggested Bob wait until his company returned, they came back depleted and exhausted, and his mates went over to the body immediately. It was obvious that they were very sad that their mate had died alone.

Bob now understands that a physical challenge that was presenting in this life had its roots in another life, he was able to positively interact in that other time and place and thus erase the imprint the trauma had made on his emotional body. Bob can now be gently caressed like any other man, without jumping out of his skin.

Career Decision

A professional jockey faced with a major career choice wished to understand something of her present situation. She explored a past life with horses in Elizabethan England, which included a graphic recall of her death as a page boy, after falling from a horse. Doubting the veracity of the scene she was presented with, I suggested she examine the horses bridle. It was unlike any thing she had ever seen or imagined. Understanding her attraction to horses and the fact that she had already died once in riding helped her make the most appropriate career move.

Angry outbursts

"Shirley" was a middle aged primary school teacher. She loved her work but was prone to outbursts of extreme anger for no real reason. Early in her session, in releasing a cellular memory relating to a pain in her heart, we discovered the cause of her anger. She had a graphic recall of being an ill equipped peasant soldier who had been knocked to the floor by a large well armoured knight with a large red cross on his tabard. He was standing over her and was about to stab her through the heart with his sword.

She was furious, when I suggested she forgive him and surrender to the perfection of her death, she just couldn't finish the affirmation. It took several attempts and at first she really didn't want to do it. After some counselling she realised it was the best thing to do. It was an emotional release and with it came the realisation that we had finally released the cause of her pent up anger.

Chronic fatigue

"Barbara" was referred to me by a local therapist who had all but given up trying to treat her ailments, which were re-presenting themselves in slightly different forms time and time again. Off the record I was told that the therapist suspected that this woman was "just plain miserable" and no amount of conventional or alternative healing could remedy the situation.

Guiding Barbara into an altered state we discovered that in her early childhood she used to pray to the Angels for help and comfort whilst her mother was busy elsewhere. This call for help and comfort was answered but not by the Angels. She was helped by another small girl who loved her very much, and was like a sister to her, protecting and guiding her. As a child she was obsessed by twin dolls always doing everything in pairs in her play. She wanted, needed and expected a twin sister in this life.

Later in life Barbara's mother revealed to her that when she was in the womb she had a pregnancy termination due to ill health. That termination was successful. However several months later she discovered she was still pregnant. Barbara was one of a pair of twins that survived the termination. The "sister" that Barbara played with was indeed the spirit of her own aborted twin, who was keen to experience life with her twin sister. Naturally when Barbara called for help she responded, not just for that time but we discovered, for the next 35 years to the present day.

Realising that her twin sister was still with her now was an emotional experience. This earthbound spirit was, with the most loving intention, preventing her from fulfilling her life's purpose by blocking her access to her own intuition or Higher Self. In order to resolve this situation Barbara's Higher Self had created these mysterious illnesses so that she would eventually, in desperation, seek the services of a spiritual healer. In this way the true cause of the imbalance could be revealed and addressed.

After counselling both the twins we agreed that it would be best if the sister returned home to light, so that she could in due course reincarnate and experience life on this plane in her own right. We also affirmed that, if it was possible, Barbara would love to nurture and help her twin when she was born again on this plane. At this point the two parted, it was a very emotional and moving experience. Also at this point all the symptoms that had been plaguing Barbara for years disappeared completely and permanently.

Sensitive therapist

"Sky" is a bright young practitioner who has decided to treat herself to experience a Crystal Dreaming. She tells me there are no particular issues that she wishes to deal with. We proceed with the session. As a sensitive individual she slips into an altered state easily.

She notices a crowd of people standing around her, they are not all happy or cheerful. A few incisive questions reveal that this woman is unintentionally acting as a host for about sixty earthbound spirits. After counselling them as a group, we assist their transit home to light, we also discover why she had attracted such an unusually large number into her aura. The bright, pure and loving light that this young woman generated whilst working with her clients was so inviting and she was so open, that these spirits just stepped from her clients to her during her sessions.

Sky had never been taught how to shield herself from spirit attachment during her sessions. Later my further research revealed that in many therapist training situations this subject ends up in the too hard (or too weird) basket and nothing is done about it. What a pity, eventually these attached spirits would have affected Sky's health emotionally, mentally and physically. Later I gave Sky some protection exercises that will prevent further spirit attachment, these include her visualising a disposable pair of gold lame gloves that she puts on before every massage and removes and places in a cleansing light after each massage.

Frozen shoulder

"Joanne" mentions that she has a stiff place in her neck and shoulder where, for as long as she can remember, energy seems to be frozen. As a trainee masseuse who is giving and swapping many sessions she tells me that her colleagues have only managed to ease this stiffness temporarily, it always returns.

As Joanne's session continued and we located her own spiritual team, we explored why her shoulder was holding frozen energy. Navigating a route through time and space we used several powerful affirmations to release the cellular memory of a past trauma being held in her neck and shoulder. As we explore this memory, Joanne becomes uneasy and apprehensive, she is having a clear past life recall of a time when she was a native African woman about to give birth. I reassure her that reliving this experience and altering how she feels about it will ease the pain in her neck and shoulder.

Neither of us have any idea what is going to come next.

We witness a difficult birth. The baby is eventually born alive and healthy but after the birth her African self continues to bleed. The local healers do their best to staunch the bleeding which lessens but does not stop. It becomes clear to everyone that she will die slowly and painfully. She says goodbye to her new baby and her husband, who loves her very much. He steps behind her, takes her head in his hands and quickly and cleanly breaks her neck. Joanne's African self knew what was coming but still the emotional trauma of her death was so great that the experience was locked into her emotional body and was manifesting in her present physical body until she was ready to deal with it.

The key to resolving this kind of past (or present) life trauma is for Joanne to be at peace with the situation. By travelling through Time and Space we are able to re-experience the event with different feelings about it. So Joanne was able to thank and forgive her husband and surrender to a peaceful and timely death knowing for sure that she would be reborn. We then travel forward in time and witness her baby grow into a healthy and strong man who honoured the memory of the mother who died bringing him into this world.

As we did this, during the session, Joanne's shoulder became unfrozen and since that day her neck and shoulder are flexible, fit and healthy.

CIA interference

An internationally known environmentalist suspected that the CIA was interfering with her psychically, to stop or discourage her crusading work in the USA. Our session revealed that there was no outside interference, in fact her own Higher Self had been attracting her attention by creating these sensations so she would have a Crystal Dreaming session. She was shown very clearly, by the spirit beings closest to her, that her work as an environmental crusader whilst worthy and valuable was not now the most appropriate or productive use of her energy.

124

She was shown that by engaging in anger in a struggle with the destroyers of our beautiful environment, she was giving them energy. She was allowing the beings manipulating this fear based reality to feed off her energy even when she was not engaged in direct conflict with them. She was advised to stop her life's work as an environmentalist and disengage her struggle. In doing so she was shown that the energy generated by her anger and despair would not be created and therefore could not be used by others. She was also shown that everything is in divine order. The whales and dolphins are volunteering to leave us, it is their choice.

She was told emphatically to focus her energies on her own well-being and to prepare herself for the inevitable planetary changes that are upon us. This was a surprise for both of us but the direction was clear, interaction with misguided or negative beings is not the most effective use of our energy.

The environmentalist agreed that she would finish her present project and then focus on her own well-being.

Crystal implant 1

"Chris" came to me because she had difficulty meditating. She had been attending meditation classes but found that as soon as she allowed herself to move into a deep space, her body contorted involuntarily with her back arching. Apart from being uncomfortable it was embarrassing and she had stopped attending classes.

As we proceeded with the session her back arched every few minutes. During the scanning process she discovered a crystal in her reproductive area. On commanding whoever placed it there to step forward she found herself having a dialogue with an ET who refused to tell her why it was there but agreed to remove it. Her body stopped arching and relaxed immediately.

Commanding her body to release the cellular memory, she discovered that she had been physically abducted, impregnated and then abducted again after a few months and the foetus removed and replaced with a crystal. I did not suggest she explored what had happened to the child.

She confided in me after the session that around the time in question she had been diagnosed as being pregnant and then the baby disappeared although she had no miscarriage.

Crystal implant 2

The client felt he had beings in his stomach all the time, he had tried releasing these beings but they would return. During the session, the client commanded his body to take him to the source of this trauma. He had a recall of a past life where he was a magician and he placed a crystal ball in his own pelvis to enhance his power at that time. This ball was a vortex of energy that created a portal to other planes of existence and allowed beings to access this reality through him. In his past lifetime he had managed to utilise their powers for his own ends. However, as the crystal had never been removed, beings were still accessing him in this life and he did not now have any control of them. They were wreaking havoc in his current life. The client had to forgive himself for creating havoc within himself, dissolve contracts with himself thus releasing the ball. Once the ball was removed the sensations slowed down but it took several sessions to release all the beings that had been using his body as each was a powerful entity that needed individual attention.

'Presence' in the room

"Judy" a judge's secretary, often felt a presence in her bedroom at night. She confided in a friend that as she fell asleep she felt that someone was sitting on the bed next to her and touching her hair. She would also sometimes wake up at night feeling pinned to the bed, as if someone was lying on top of her. Also when she visited her mother, her mum's cat, normally an affectionate animal, would head in the opposite direction when she arrived and not go anywhere near her.

During her session she had a clear perception of a man in the room close to us. He was very happy that she could see him and talk to him, in fact he was deeply in love with her and had been for about four hundred years. He was a lover from a past life who had been following her around for several years trying to attract her attention. He could not understand why she could not see him or remember who he was. In their past life together he had become obsessed with her and she had rejected his love. Broken hearted he had committed suicide vowing that he would never leave her. So he followed her around for the rest of that life until she died, staying here as an earthbound spirit waiting for her to reincarnate. He found her again several years ago and had been trying to attract her attention ever since.

We explained that Judy could not reciprocate his love as she was here in another body having another lifetime and his presence was stifling her growth here now. I asked him if he truly loved her, he said yes he did. In which case, I suggested, he would understand that she should be free to grow and be happy without him. I reassured him that they would meet again after Judy leaves her body at the end of this lifetime and he reluctantly agreed to go home to light. After an emotional farewell, I called on his spirit guides to come and assist with his journey home. Judy was very relieved and considering she had no conscious recall of their affair, she was also quite teary.

The evening visits ceased and next time she visited her mum the cat jumped straight onto her lap and started purring.

Scarred arms

During a training session I was describing how if trauma is not released at the appropriate time then the body will help by drawing attention to it through repeated injuries to the part of the body where the trauma is held.

One of the students went pale and said "Oh my God" I asked her what was happening, she stood up and showed the class her arms. They were covered in cuts, bruises, scalds and scars. She told us no sooner had she healed from one minor accident then another happened. I suggested it was likely she would find out what it was all about when she received a practice session the following day.

During the session which was facilitated by another student and supervised by myself, she quickly released the trauma and it was major. In the scan she noticed her arms appeared to be wrapped in barbed wire and she commanded her body to release the cellular memory. She had a graphic recall of being a Jewess in a Nazi prisoner of war camp. She was raped, tortured and then dragged behind a truck with her arms wrapped in barbed wire. Naturally she was terrified as it was a horribly traumatic death.

Even though the pain and trauma were physical it was the emotional trauma that needed to be released. She forgave the soldiers who were abusing her, the Nazis in general and Adolf Hitler in particular. This she did with some difficulty and as she did so her body completely relaxed.

After the session she told me that for her whole life she had felt afraid and never knew why. She no longer felt afraid. She also said that a long standing heart condition completely disappeared after the session. Her arms are no longer accident prone.

Disco inferno

In another student practice session the student released a traumatic memory that did not appear to make sense at first. She had a graphic recall of being in an Asian country having a fun time in a disco when a ball of flame engulfed the whole place after an explosion and she was killed. We checked the environment for clues to the time and place. It was very recent, much too recent for her to have died and been reborn.

What was confusing for the student facilitator was that she was obviously experiencing a traumatic "past life" death in the then recent, Bali terrorist bombings in which many Australians were killed. It could not have been a past life.

As she was in distress I encouraged the student practitioner to release the trauma as if it was past life, which she did, much to everyone's relief. Later in the session after the client had connected with her team I asked them to explain.

They told us that a close member of her soul family (who she had never met in the flesh) was killed in the Bali Bombings. On the highest level, knowing that a "family" member was in training and about to experience a Crystal Dreaming session the clients higher self and her entire team agreed that she would release the trauma in the training session to facilitate growth for all concerned. Because of the oneness of her family, she experienced and released the trauma first hand.

A simpler way of understanding this could be to accept that her higher self was having several incarnations simultaneously and that one of them was killed in Bali. As they both came directly from the same consciousness the student was able to release the trauma as if she had experienced it personally. Even though it was not past life and it did not appear to be her.

As there are multiple realities existing side by side, the trauma could even have come from a parallel reality in which she was killed. However trauma presents itself, if the client is experiencing it first hand then treat it as a first hand trauma release, you can discover more from their team later, after the release.

Vietnam Veteran

In another training session a Vietnam Veteran had a graphic recall of trauma in this life. As a young man he was conscripted into the army and served in the Vietnam war. As a non-professional soldier he found himself poorly prepared in some terrifying situations.

His platoon were forced behind enemy lines and he had to wade through a crocodile infested river up to his neck, in full kit, in total darkness. The extreme fear the young man went through left him open to attachment and at that point he attracted a Demon of fear, which had played havoc with his life ever since.

Confronting this aggressive Demon during the session was terrifying for the client and the student facilitator. Being a novice, the student had overlooked his training and decided that the best way to force the demon to release its grip on the client was to encourage the client to bring in more light which was unpleasant for the Demon. The client did as instructed but this only then put the demon in a state of further agitation and fear. It tightened its grip on the veteran.

By the time I stepped into the session to assist the client was literally being picked up off the ground by invisible claws and was screaming as they were digging into his arms. I instructed the client to wind back the level of light and enter a dialogue with the demon telling it how beautiful it was. It did not take long for the Demon to realise it was a being of light, release the client and go home to light; a much gentler and easier way of dealing with the situation.

Refer to my book "Spirit World" for further case studies.

Endword

As long as you describe the technique you offer to your clients as Crystal Dreaming™ you must stick with the protocols described in this book. You may only refer to your sessions as Crystal Dreaming™ after proper training in person from a certified teacher; please acknowledge the source of your work. Do not teach others without formal certified teacher training with myself.

As you become more confident, trust your inner guidance. If you are working from unconditional love, you cannot go wrong. Practice will revive the dormant memory within you, so practise.

After a year's practice you may consider the Advanced Crystal Dreaming course which I offer in person to selected practitioners.

The range of healings that you will facilitate in your Crystal Dreaming journeys will be profound and beautiful. Working with crystals as your allies you are able to tackle many of the insoluble health challenges your clients may be faced with, particularly those stubborn and mysterious conditions that appear to refuse all other forms of treatment, conventional or complementary. The answer to these mysterious ailments is not in physical treatment; it lies in higher dimensions of the spirit realm, a place that your client can access easily and safely with your help.

The focus of Crystal Dreaming is the empowerment of clients to diagnose and treat themselves, implementing positive life changes from knowledge they personally have retrieved from the spirit realm. Anyone can do this, it is our birthright. We are all infinitely powerful spirit beings, temporarily inhabiting physical bodies in this third dimension. You may understand, live and apply this Universal truth through Crystal Dreaming.

In the course of your work in this area you will meet many challenges and you will be ready for each one as it arrives. For all the challenging situations you will encounter there will be many more exquisite reunions with The Source; life transforming insights, profound emotional and spiritual healings and physical transformations into wholeness, wellness and peace.

Reunification with The Source can positively transform anyone's life. You will facilitate that sweet and elusive connection many times and you will be moved to tears yourself by the presence of absolute joy and unconditional love your clients will experience.

To share this path with you is my honour and privilege.

Namasté,

Raym.

Recommended reading and viewing

Reading

Spirit Guide	Raym
Spirit World	Raym
The Book of Stones	Robert Simmons & Naisha Ahsian
Love is in the Earth	Melody
Crystal Workbook/Checklist	Sherril Berkovitch
Crystal Enlightenment	Katrina Raphaell
Crystal Bible	Judy Hall
The Only Planet of Choice	Phyllis Schemmer
ET 101	Mission Control
The Pleiadian Agenda	Barbara Hand Clow
The Bringers of the Dawn	Barbara Marciniak
Earth, Pleiadian Keys to the Living Library	Barbara Marciniak
Basic Pranic Healing	Choa Kok Sui
An Ascension Handbook	Tony Stubbs
The Chakra Handbook	S.Sharamon and B.J.Baginski
Nothing in this Book is True...	Bob Frissel
The Keys of Enoch	J J Hurtak
Earth's Birth Changes	St. Germain
The Ancient secret of the Flower of Life 1&2	Drunvalo Melchizedek

Viewing

2001 A Space Odyssey	The Fifth Element
Contact	Thrive
Lord of the Rings	Dune
What planet are you from?	What Dreams May Come
The Matrix	Solaris
The Race to Zero Point	Cloud Atlas
What the Bleep do we know?	Dr Strange
Gravity	Inception

The Mists of Avalon (TV series)	Outlander (TV series)
Humans (UK TV series)	

Questions and affirmations

Preparing your client

"How do you feel?"

"How was your journey here?"

"How did you sleep last night?"

"Why have you come to see me?"

"Have you experienced any major trauma in your life?"

Promises

"I promise to speak with you at all times during the session. I promise to return to my physical body at the end of this session when you call me back. I authorise you to intercede on my behalf should it become necessary."

Invocation

"I call on _____'s Higher Self. I call on _____'s spiritual guides, teachers and friends. Please be with us today. Please share with us your healing energies and protection.

I call on my own Higher Self. I call on my own Mastery. I call on my Spiritual guides, teachers and friends. I call on the beings who love us unconditionally. Please be with us today. Please share with us your healing energies and protection. I ask in full faith. So be it."

Column of light and cleansing

Do NOT use the words *visualise* or *imagine*!

*"**Become aware of** a column of light above your head. It stretches up through the clouds, into the stars and beyond, back to the Source of all light, the source of all love. It is uninterrupted Divine energy, a vibrant golden white light. It pours down on your head and shoulders and follows you everywhere, like a spotlight. (Pause).*

Now notice a white flower with many petals on top of your head. Allow the flower to open as if to the morning sun. As it opens, gently breathe light in through the flower from the column above your head into your body. (Pause).

As you breathe light in through the flower allow it to pick up any negative thoughts or feelings and take them down towards the feet. Open a tap or valve in the centre of each foot just below the ball of each foot. As you breathe out allow the old energy out, returning to Mother Earth. With each breath draw more light into your body from the column above, sparkling and tingling, gently caressing and filling your body with light. As you breath out, release any excess energy through the open valves in your feet."

Plunging

"Create a disk of light as wide as your body hovering above the top of your head. Fill the disk with light from the column above. When it is as full and bright, take a deep breath in and on the out breath plunge the disk down through your body like a coffee plunger."

Repeat - emerald green, royal blue and iridescent violet discs.

Full body X-Ray

"Look down on your body from above, you have CAT scan or X-ray eyes. Using all your senses, looking, feeling, sensing, scan the energy inside and around your body starting above the head and working all the way down to below the feet. As you work your way down through your body tell me if you notice anything unusual or uncomfortable. (You can also do this by feeling)."

*"What do you **perceive**?"*

With affirmations, when possible

"Across Time and Space..."

"Of my own free will..."

"In full consciousness..."

"As the Universe is my witness..."

"NOW."

For those having difficulty

"How do you feel?"

"What is the heavy thing on your chest made of?"

"What kind of environment are you in?"

"Feel your body, what is it like?"

"What are wearing?"

"What is causing the sharp pain in your back, feel into it, what is it made of?"

"What is the ball in your throat made of? What colour is it?"

Spirit attachment

"I am aware of your presence, what do you want? Show yourself to me now. Don't be afraid, I promise not to hurt you."

"What year is it? Do you realise you are dead?"

"It is now the twenty first century. Your body is long gone. There is a much nicer place to go to than staying here with me. Please let me help you."

"I call on this person's spirit guides, I call on this person's spirit guides, I call on this person's spirit guides.

Please come close to us and help this person journey home to light and find peace. Now."

Clearing energy

"Draw light through the open flower on your crown, from the inexhaustible source above your head. Take it down through your heart, mix it with unconditional love, then to ... (the area to be cleared). With each out-breath, gently push out thousands of pinpricks of light into the area of discomfort. Observe what happens."

Cellular memory

"I give myself permission to remember exactly what happened to me: body show me now."

"Body I command you take me to the moment this happened."

"Body I command you release the cellular memory I am holding here, into full consciousness now. Show me exactly what happened. Now."

"I dissolve any agreements I have made with myself for my own protection. I choose to remember what happened to me now"

"I dissolve any agreements I have made with any other being regarding remembering what happened to me. Body I command you take me to the moment this started. Now."

Forgiveness

"Across Time and Space I call on the beings responsible for my death/torture/humiliation. Please stand before me now."

"I forgive you, I forgive you, I forgive you. With all my heart I freely forgive you.

In forgiving you I release you from this trauma, as I release myself, to find joy, peace, happiness and freedom. Go in peace, thank you.

This trauma no longer binds us. You are released, go in peace."

"I surrender to the perfection of this death. Everything is perfect,

all my choices are perfect. My choice to experience this event has served me well and I have learnt a great deal from it and do not need to repeat it. I forgive anyone who has harmed me.

It was OK to feel the way I did when I had this experience, but I choose now to leave it in the past where it belongs. I leave all feelings of guilt/despair/grief etc in the past where they belong. This experience now ceases to have any power over me as I release it to be transmuted into light, for the divine highest good of all."

Soul retrieval

"I call upon the beings that love me unconditionally (x3). Please be here now and assist me in releasing this fragmented part of myself to be absorbed into oneness and bliss. Please return this fragmented part of my being to unity consciousness so that I may become integrated, whole and complete, now."

Repair

"Drawing light in through the crown from the inexhaustible source above your head, take it through the heart centre mixing it with unconditional love, rebuilding and repairing the heart, opening a beautiful pink flower there."

ETs and implants

"Body show me the moment this was placed here, take me there now."

"You must remove this now, I no longer need it and you do not have my permission to leave this here. Thank you for allowing me to look after it for you, I no longer need it. Please remove it now and go in peace."

"You know this is a free will zone and you may not leave it here without my consent. You no longer have my consent, please remove it now. Thank you."

"Thank you for removing it, go in peace. You may not return without my conscious written permission."

"You must leave me now, our agreement is complete, you no longer have my permission be here. Thank you for teaching me my limitations, go in peace. You are released."

"You know this is a free will zone and you may not stay here without my consent. You no longer have my consent, please leave now. Thank you."

"Thank you for helping me and coming when I asked you to. Our agreement is now complete. I have learnt all I need to know about... (fear etc.) You no longer have my permission to be here. Please leave me now and go in peace. You know you cannot stay without my conscious written permission. I am a sovereign being of light, I reclaim my sovereignty, I reclaim my power, I reclaim my freedom. Go in peace. Now!"

Go up the chain of command if necessary

Ask to see the ETs supervisor and keep going until you find one that understands this is a free will zone and they cannot implant people without their conscious permission. Be courteous and polite at all times.

"Thank you for removing it, go in peace. You may not return without my conscious written permission."

Implanted crystals

"Whoever placed this here, show yourself to me. Now!"

"What is our relationship? Why did you place this here?"

"Thank you for leaving it there, it has served me well. I have learnt a great deal from looking after it, but I no longer need it. You can remove it now, it has been an honour looking after it for you."

Entities

"I am aware of your presence, show yourself to me and tell me what you want."

"Don't be afraid, I promise not to hurt you. I would like to thank you, I can help you. Step forward and tell me what you want."

"Thank you for your service, our agreement is now complete and is no longer binding. You are released from it. You are free now to go home to light, I can help you if you wish. Would you like that?"

"I call on the beings that love this being unconditionally, I call on the beings that love this being unconditionally, I call on the beings that love this being unconditionally. Please come close to us now and help this being go home and find peace."

Fear

"As the Universe is my witness, I choose to live in a fear free environment. I acknowledge my fear as a powerful friend that makes me alert and ready for action, and I thank it for serving me. However, fear does not control me.

I choose to centre myself in love and light, I choose to live love, be and share love. Nothing has power over me on this or any other plane. I am a sovereign being of light, my power is limitless. I choose peace, I chose joy, I choose love. Now."

Final plunge

"Create another disk of light above your head. Compress the light above your head into a disk that is as wide as your body. When it is full and bright take a deep in breath in and on the out breath plunge it slowly down through the body taking time to thank every part of your physical body for enabling you to have this is experience here on Earth now."

The waterfall

"Take yourself to a beautiful place in nature, where there is a crystal clear waterfall and rock pool. Go and stand under the waterfall and allow it to wash over you, cleansing every part of your body. Move your body round and make sure every part of your body is cleansed. Take a moment to honour the beautiful being of light that you are.

How does that feel?

When you feel cleansed and refreshed step out of the waterfall and have a look around, tell me about the place you are in. Describe it to me...

I am interested to know if you notice anything particularly interesting or beautiful..."

Useful questions

"What is happening now?"

"What kind of space are you in?"

"How do you feel?"

"What is your body like, is it male or female?"

"What is the solid ball in your throat made of? What colour is it?"

"What is our relationship? "(With a being just encountered).

"Do you love me?"

"Do you love me unconditionally?"

"What do you want?"

"When did I give you permission to be here?"

"What is the nature of our agreement?"

"I can help you, don't be afraid."

With guides...

"Please take me into a deeper state so I may hear and see you more clearly."

"Please check everything we have done today and ensure that all my bodies, in all realities are now completely clear."

"Providing you love me unconditionally I ask and give permission for you to remove all energies not totally aligned with unconditional love, now."

"Show me when we spent time together and what we did together. I have completely forgotten."

"Please take me to a sacred place. I am ready to remember all that I am.... Please re-initiate me as the High Priestess that I am"

"I am ready to activate my life plan in service to light and unconditional love. Please show me what changes I should make in my life now to allow this to flow with ease and grace."

"Providing you love me unconditionally, I give my permission for you to guide and protect me, stay close to me, be with me in my meditations and dreams."

Bringing someone back who refuses to return

"I am placing grounding stones on your body which will bring you back. You are returning to your body now, the crystals around your body have been removed, it is time to come back now."

Karmic court

"I now request a hearing at the Karmic court.

Approach the court with respect. Advise them we are here to plead your case. We are requesting the Karma we have just become aware of now be considered to be cleared.

You have been totally forgiven by those involved and all ties to the trauma have been voluntarily released by all parties concerned.

We now respectfully plead clemency, please release me from this Karma."

Spontaneous past life recall

How does your body feel? Is it male or female?"

"Look down at your body, what are you wearing?"

"Tell me what is going on around you, how are people dressed?

138

What are they doing? What tools are they using?"

"Do you recognise anyone's energy?"

Dissolving blocks

"I now dissolve all agreements I may have made with myself for my own protection."

"I now dissolve all agreements that may have been made on my behalf before I was born."

"I now dissolve all agreements I may have made or that have been made on my behalf with any circle or society in a past life relating to my lineage. I revoke all past life contracts that are not part of my Divine plan or totally aligned with light."

"I challenge any being that is under the illusion that it has power over me show yourself to me NOW!"

Everything is perfect

"Everything is perfect, I honour my choice to have (or witness) this experience. I understand that I know nothing of the Divine plan and where this may lead and I accept that everything is perfect. All my choices were perfect. I thank my cells for retaining this memory, it has served its purpose, I now accept all that I am.

I now affirm that I no longer need to hold on to this memory as it no longer serves me. I release this cellular memory now, to be transmuted into light for the divine highest good of all. So be it!"

Aggressive entities

"Don't be afraid, no one here wants to hurt you or trick you. There is no retribution where you are going, only peace and love."

Breaking all agreements

"I_____ of my own free will now dissolve any and all agreements I may have made consciously or unconsciously, with any negative energy or entity, earthbound spirit, alien or reptoid on any plane at any time. Thank you for your service, thank you for teaching me my limitations, thank you for helping me grow, I no longer need you. Please leave me now, please go to the light with love, or show yourself to me and tell me what you want, NOW!"

"Don't be afraid I promise not to harm you."

Curses and spells

"Drawing light through the crown, take it down to your power

centre or Hara, a hands breadth below the navel in the centre of your body. There build a star pushing out light with every out breath. Allow it to grow filling your body, pushing out shafts of light in every direction, dissolving any energies not totally aligned with light.

When your body is full of light, extend light beyond your body, creating an egg-shape all around you. Allow that to fill with light.

When the egg is complete, see yourself bathing in a cool violet flame, then see a violet flame licking the outside of your egg, leaving a violet hue.

When that feels comfortable create a sparkling gold see-through criss-cross mesh on the outside of the egg and then create a platinum mesh on top of that. You may declare that this mesh will only let love and light in and will repel all other thought forms.

Project a ray of pink from your own heart projecting unconditional love for all things. Allow that to spread out from your heart, forming a bubble that surrounds your whole being.

Now create a mirror ball on the outside of your egg, there should be small spaces between the mirrors which completely cover your egg. Then place a supercharged coating of unconditional love on the mirror which you instruct to reflect any negative intentions back to the sender, along with unconditional love and wishes for enlightenment.

You may now declare out loud:

"I am light,
I am love,
I am protected."

Demons

"You have no power over me, you never have had any power over me, you never will have any power over me. Across time and space as the Universe is my witness, I reclaim my power, I reclaim my freedom.

Thank you for your service, thank you for teaching me my limitation. Our agreement is now complete. I have learned all I need to know about fear/despair/anger etc.

I now dissolve all agreements with you. I am a being of light, I am a being of love, I am inviolate, I am that I am, I am a free Spirit! So be it."

"In you I see great light, in you I see great beauty.

You are a beautiful being of light, you are loved. You always were loved you always will be loved.

Look inside yourself, to your core, tell me what you see.

You are beautiful."

Ritual abuse

"I forgive you, I forgive you, I forgive you. With all my heart I freely forgive you.

I forgive you for torturing and abusing me as a child.

In forgiving you I release you from this trauma, as I release myself, to find joy, peace, happiness and freedom. Go in peace, thank you.

We are no longer bound by this trauma. You are released, go in peace."

"I call on the being I was forced to marry, I call on the being who raped me, please stand before me now.

All agreements between us are now dissolved. You have no power over me, you never have had any power over me, you never will have any power over me.

Thank you for teaching me my limitations, I forgive you for abusing me. Our relationship is complete. Go in peace, you are now released from all agreements. They no longer bind us. Be at peace.

You may not return without my conscious written permission."

Also if needed:

"The ritual marriage I was forced into was not entered into with my free will and cannot therefore be binding. I dissolve all vows I made under duress, now. The agreement we entered into is null and void and no longer binds us. I am a free spirit, so be it. Go in peace."

Returning to the Source

"Of my own free will, I now request a merging with the source of all Light, the source of all Love. Please take me there now, I am ready to merge with it and experience oneness with All There Is, NOW!"

Ending session

"Notice a rainbow nearby and to fly into it or ask your team to lift you up and place you in it. Float in it's colours, allowing the colours to balance, harmonise and energise your body. Allow yourself to slide down the rainbow and slip back into your physical body through the top of their head.

Feeling fingers, toes, bones, muscles, breath, crystals on your body, gently stretching, slowly open your eyes and become fully present here with me."

I give thanks to _____ 's spiritual guides, teachers and friends. I give thanks to my own spiritual guides, teachers and friends, my own mastery and my own Higher Self. Thank you all for being with us today. Thank you for sharing with us, your healing energies and protection. I give thanks, in full faith. So be it."

Post session discussion

"Any questions? Anything you did not understand?

Do not drive immediately after a session. Take a walk, have a snack.

You may feel tired this evening take it easy, pamper yourself."

Reset the journey

If a client perceives nothing in the scan after several attempts, focussing on feeling as well as seeing, you may take them straight to the waterfall. The scan is the short cut, they will meet and clear whatever they need to after the waterfall.

If a client is not experiencing the other side of the waterfall as expected or if the client has released trauma and is in "no time-space" you can reset the journey at any time by taking them back to the waterfall, bathing, cleansing and stepping out into a (usually) different environment..

If the waterfall is not working for the client they can visit any place that they feel comfortable in. Take the journey from there, looking for things that look interesting or beautiful. If they know the place ask them to look out for anything different or unusual and to explore the environment beyond their memory.

Weird and unexpected

If things go pear shaped, remember that this is happening to you because you can deal with it. Take a deep breath and think about how you can help the client apply forgiveness and compassion in the situation they are experiencing or the entity they are dealing with.

Aggressive entities that appear to be very powerful are all ultimately looking to experience unconditional love. You can help them, be patient and do not be intimidated.

You are an extraordinarily powerful being, easily as powerful as *any* you will encounter.

Crystal Dreaming™ Mandala

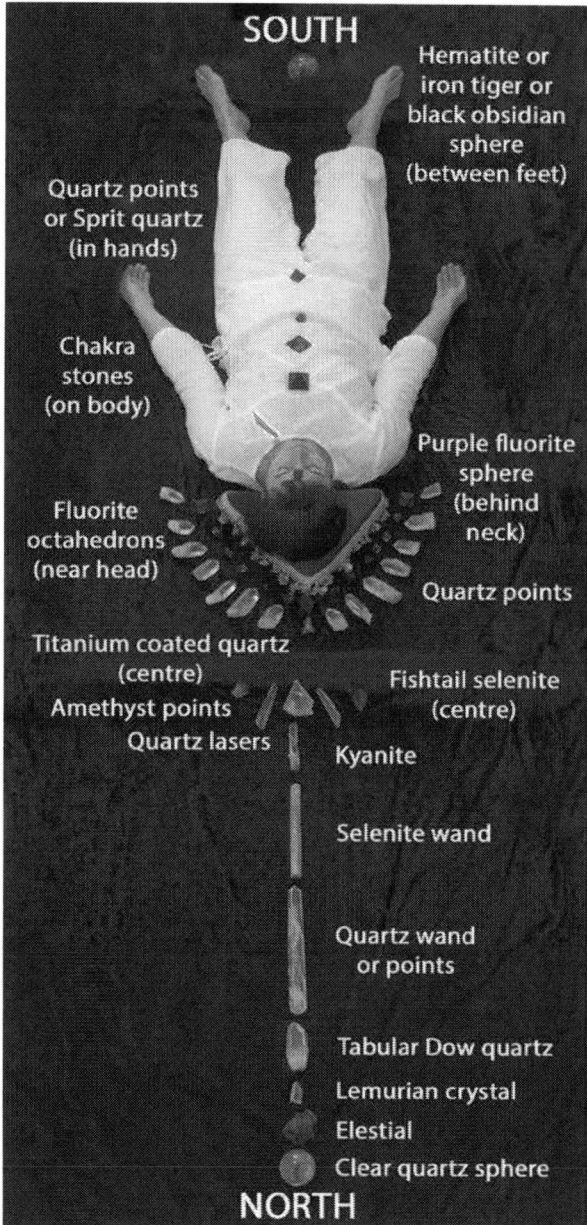

SOUTH

Hematite or iron tiger or black obsidian sphere (between feet)

Quartz points or Sprit quartz (in hands)

Chakra stones (on body)

Purple fluorite sphere (behind neck)

Fluorite octahedrons (near head)

Quartz points

Titanium coated quartz (centre)

Fishtail selenite (centre)

Amethyst points

Quartz lasers

Kyanite

Selenite wand

Quartz wand or points

Tabular Dow quartz

Lemurian crystal

Elestial

Clear quartz sphere

NORTH

Crystal Dreaming™ synopsis

Centre and clear yourself.

Clear your healing space.

Invoke your team.

Prepare the space, layout your crystals, head to the North.

Welcome your client.

How are you? How did you sleep?

How was your journey here? Do you have any phobias?

Why have you come to see me? Are you on any medication?

Have you experienced any major trauma in your life?

Lie your client down, ball under neck, crystals in hands.

Invoke for guidance, invite your clients team to participate.

Ask permission to intervene on their behalf if necessary.

Client promises to talk to you and return.

Client closes eyes now.

Perceive column, open a lotus flower on top of the head.

Draw light in through the crown and open valves in feet.

Plunge clear, green, blue and violet light.

Scan/x-ray from above, any unusual or uncomfortable energies?

What do you perceive? Using all your senses.

Clear blockages, cellular memory and trauma release, entities.

Forgiveness!

Waterfall, bathe and cleanse step out, look around.

What do you *percieve*? NO suggestions!

Do not lead your client. Open ended questions.

Explore environment, anything beautifull attracts attention?

More clearing if required.

Contact guides! First they check all your work, any questions?

Ask guides to help client access a deeper state if needed.

What is your clients life plan, any special gifts from other lives?

Anyone else to meet, Higher Self, teacher, Ascended Master?

Merge with Higher Self or Oneness, source of all light and love.

Any gifts from team? Light codes, DNA activation, past life skills.

How can client access their team after session?

Tools/gifts from their team?

Return via rainbow, give thanks to both teams.

Made in the USA
Columbia, SC
29 October 2017